# Glory on the Hilltop

## The Story of 1947 SMU Football

### By T. R. Williams

*Inspired Forever Book Publishing*
*Irving, Texas*

Glory on the Hilltop: The Story of 1947 SMU Football
© 2017 T. R. Williams

*All rights reserved*, including the right of reproduction in whole or in part in any form without prior written permission, except in the case of brief quotations embodied in critical reviews and certain other noncommercial uses permitted by copyright law.

Inspired Forever Book Publishing™
"Bringing Inspiration to Print"
Irving, Texas
(888) 403-2727

Printed in the United States of America
Library of Congress Control Number: 2017960365
Softcover ISBN-13: 978-0-9996258-0-4

For more information about the author and book, visit:
www.gloryonthehilltopthebook.com

*Glory on the Hilltop* is dedicated to the 1947 SMU varsity football team, their coaches, and the 1947 SMU cheerleaders.

# Contents

Preface: Tall Tales .................................................................... vii

One: High on the Hilltop ............................................................ 1

Two: 1947 College Football Season ........................................... 11

Three: Ewell Doak Walker, Jr. .................................................... 21

Four: William Madison Bell ....................................................... 29

Five: Joe Redwine Patterson ..................................................... 37

Six: 1947 Mustang Players ........................................................ 51

Seven: SMU Spirit and Cheerleaders ........................................ 81

Eight: Mustang Assistant Coaches ........................................... 99

Nine: 1947 SMU Season .......................................................... 105

Ten: 1948 Cotton Bowl ............................................................ 137

Eleven: More than Just a Game ............................................... 149

Twelve: The Leakage of Time .................................................. 155

Conclusion: The Best SMU Football Season ............................ 163

Postscript: The Reality of the 2015 SMU Football Season ....... 165

Appendix A – SMU Football Roster, 1947 ............................... 173

Appendix B – SMU Demographics .......................................... 177

Appendix C – SMU Football Demographics ........................... 179

Appendix D – SMU Football Home Attendance Comparison .... 181

Acknowledgements ................................................................ 183

Sources ................................................................................... 185

Index ....................................................................................... 189

# Preface: Tall Tales

The friendship started during a typical game of handball on handball court No. 3 at the old downtown Dallas YMCA and it lasted for forty-six years. Over the course of those forty-six years, I heard a lot of what I thought were tall tales. There were stories of growing up in small North Texas towns and milking the family cow in the backyard. There were stories of boxing an orphan from the Ft. Worth Masonic Home in the Golden Gloves. Most of the tales, however, were stories regarding Southern Methodist University (SMU) and the special magic of the 1947 SMU football season.

Joe Redwine Patterson had lots of SMU football stories, especially about Doak Walker, one player on the 1947 team. Patterson claimed that in a 1947 game, he had seen Walker, as a defensive back, running faster backward than his covered receiver was running forward. As Head SMU Cheerleader, Patterson claimed that agitated SMU World War II veterans had thrown beer cans at him as he stood on the steps of Dallas Hall during an SMU pep rally. Patterson talked about being over-run and driven to the ground by The Fighting Texas Aggie Band at halftime of the 1947 SMU/A&M football game. He spoke of being in the locker room at halftime of SMU football games and hearing Head Coach Matty Bell give the halftime instructions to players. But most of all, Patterson spoke of the 1947 Spirit of SMU and how that Spirit developed during the 1947 football season. In 2010, Patterson, in his words, was on a mission "to restore the school spirit mechanism." Patterson never accomplished that goal. As many an old man has mused, Patterson once lamented, "I learned that you can never go back." Greek philosopher, Heraclitus, said it best," We cannot step into the same river twice."

*Glory on the Hilltop* documents the 1947 SMU football season. The book also describes the SMU world of 1947 that is so vastly different than the world of SMU today. Much has changed on the Hilltop, but one thing has stayed the same. A renovated Dallas Hall still "towers on the hill over there."

# Chapter One
# High on the Hilltop

The alma mater story becomes a little hazy as facts merge with myths over time. In 1916, as one story goes, theology student Louis N. Stuckey had had one of those bad days as a student pastor where nothing had gone right in his small churches in Farmers Branch and Carrollton, Texas. In an interview with the Semi-Weekly Campus on March 5, 1924, Stuckey recalled, "I was coming into school over Preston Road. For miles, I could see the university ahead of me. Feeling fine, I went to singing. How I do not know, but somehow, the words and music of Varsity just naturally came together and by the time I stopped the car in front of the administration building the song was composed." Stuckey had penned the following four lines of verse:

"Oh, we see the Varsity, Varsity, Varsity,
As she towers o'er the hill over there,
And our hearts are filled with joy, SMU, SMU,
Alma Mater we'll be true forever."

Later in the spring of 1916, a good friend of Stuckey, Harrison Baker, came to visit Stuckey in Carrollton. The two sang the song several times during Baker's visit. As president of the SMU Glee Club, Baker shared the song with Harold Hart Todd, who organized the first SMU band. It took thirteen years, but in 1929, Varsity was named the official school song of SMU. The SMU Glee Club was the first group to sing Varsity publicly. What was it that inspired Stuckey to be so overjoyed that day in 1916? Only Stuckey knows for sure. SMU historians, however, do know that SMU's Dallas Hall's dome above the clouds would give Stuckley enough passion for the words and tune of Varsity. One-hundred years later, SMU students and alumni are still singing that short song that popped into the head of an SMU theology student so long ago.

## SMU in the 1940s

In the 1940s, SMU had grown into more than just the vision of a single building on a hilltop on the North Dallas plain. In 1947, the student body numbered approximately 6,700 students. Because of the GI Bill, a large percentage of the SMU student body included soldiers and sailors returning from service after enlisting in the armed forces. The former GIs lived in a cluster of prefabricated houses named "Trailerville," which was located near the southern end of Bishop Boulevard. Various articles described the miserable life for students living in Trailerville. These students complained about lack of hot water and insignificant heating. Trailerville was not to be confused with "the Barracks," which housed additional men on the somewhat barren SMU campus.

The World War II veterans and the non-veteran students came to SMU with totally different life experiences. For the veterans after being on the other side of the world, fighting for their lives, and seeing their friends killed or wounded was a life-changing experience. It was especially hard for veterans to get excited about cheering for a football team. However, many of the SMU football

A Completed Dallas Hall circa 1919

starters were veterans themselves, and several campus leaders were also veterans.

The underlying reason the Dallas veterans came back home rather than choosing a college in another city was a strong urge to return to the familiar. As Dorothy said in "The Wizard of Oz," "There is no place like home." Therefore, it is not surprising that approximately 62% of the SMU graduating class of 1948 were from Dallas proper. That number didn't include students from the Dallas suburbs, such as Richardson, Garland, or Grand Prairie.

## Reflections from the SMU *Rotunda*

The format and presentation of material in the 1948 SMU *Rotunda* (the SMU Annual Yearbook) reflect the changes to the SMU student body that have occurred over the past seventy years. The student clubs listed in the *Rotundas* in 1948 and 2016 can be found on page 5.

It's interesting to note that the number of clubs listed for both the 1948 and the 2016 *Rotundas* are approximately the same. In addition, no student organizations from 1948 still existed in 2016, and all the clubs based on religious preference were gone. In 2016, there is less emphasis on students' hometowns, and individual student pictures in the *Rotunda* do not even list their hometowns. The clubs of the 2016 *Rotunda* seem to focus on students' special interests. Anyone wishing to form a club on today's campus a student just has to find two or three other students with the same special interest. Once a student organizes a club, the club's picture is in the *Rotunda*.

*The Glory of "Trailerville" circa 1947*

On the social side of the spectrum, SMU had twelve fraternities and twelve sororities in 1947. However, only five sororities have full-page spreads and only one fraternity has a full-page presentation in the 2016 *Rotunda*. However, the Sing-Song singing competition includes the names of additional fraternities and sororities.

In 1947, there were approximately twenty-six permanent buildings and structures on the SMU campus. There were only two women's dorms on campus, Snyder Hall, and Virginia Hall, which housed approximately 213 women. The only permanent men's dorm was Atkins Hall, which housed approximately 172 men. All dorm students had to eat meals in the dorm cafeterias. Dorm guests were charged $2 per day for room and board, and parents of students were charged only after the third day of a campus visit. Freshman men were required to live with relatives if they lived off campus, and no freshman men could live in fraternity houses. All women students had to live in dorms unless they were living with nearby relatives. In an *SMU Campus* article, the total number of housed students on campus was 670, which included men housed in the temporary veteran dormitories, Mustang Manor, and the athletic dorm. There were also twenty-six temporary housing structures in 1947.

Religion was a big part of SMU education in 1947. All SMU students were expected to attend "divine worship" at least once each Sunday in the church of their choice. The chapel was mandatory for students majoring in Arts & Science, Engineering, and Business

## Student Clubs Listed in the *Rotundas*

| 1948 | 2016 |
| --- | --- |
| Alpha Kappa Psi | Alpha Epsilon Delta |
| Alpha Phi Omega | Alpha Kappa Alpha Sorority |
| American Legion | Alternative Breaks |
| Arkansas Club | Black Men Emerging |
| American Society of Civil Engineers | College Hispanic American Students |
| American Society of Mechanical Engineers | Chinese Student Union |
| | Association of Black Students |
| Beta Kappa Gamma | Association of Latino Professionals |
| The Blue Shirts | Club Volleyball |
| Baptist Student Union | Delta Sigma Theta Sorority |
| Canterbury Club | East Asian Student Association |
| Clef Club | Habitat for Humanity |
| COGS | Honor Council |
| Delta Commerce Club | Intervarsity Christian Fellowship |
| Delta Phi Alpha | Marketing Association |
| Delta Psi Kappa | McNair Scholars Program |
| Delta Theta Phi | Medieval Club |
| SMU Geographic Society | Mustang Fitness Club |
| Hillel Counsellorship | National Residence Hall Honorary |
| The Houston Club | National Society of Black Engineers |
| Iota Pi Alpha | National Society of Collegiate Scholar |
| Kirkos | |
| Les Honores | Polo Club |
| The Methodist Student Movement | Program Council |
| | Robotics Club |
| Mu Phi Epsilon | Sigma Lambda Beta |
| Phi Alpha Delta | Sigma Lambda Gamma |
| Presbyterian Students' Association | Sisters Supporting Sisters |
| | Society of Automotive Engineers |
| Psi Chi | Society of Women Engineers |
| Sigma Delta Chi | Southern Gentlemen |
| St. Mary's Catholic Club | Theta Tau Engineering Fraternity |
| Theta Sigma Phi | Tunes for Texas |
| The Van Katwijk Club | United Student's Association |
| Women's Self-Governing Board | Voices of the Animals |
| Zeta Phi Eta | |

Administration. However, the frequency of chapel attendance and the monitoring of SMU student worship attendance were not described in the Student Handbook.

All students were required to have a physical exam by an SMU physician. Vaccinations also were required for all new students. The school year started in late September and ended in late May, and included a two-week break for Christmas. Final fall exams were taken at the end of January the following year.

In the 21st century, SMU made an effort to encourage more sophomores and juniors to live on campus. The purpose was to instill a larger sense of community among the students and to promote a sense of competition among the eleven residential commons. Students were equally interested in the spirit of competition to earn the Commons Cup as to participate in intercollegiate team sports. As reflected in the 2016 *Rotunda*, additional housing options for upperclassman included Daniel House, Martin Hall, Moore Hall, and SMU Service House.

## Intercollegiate Sports

The 1948 *Rotunda* devoted twenty-eight pages to the SMU football teams and players, and twelve pages to the SMU basketball team. The men's swimming team and the cheerleaders each had one page, and the men's and women's intramural teams had seven pages. In 1947, there were no women's intercollegiate sports teams at SMU.

*Rotunda* pages of SMU intercollegiate sports in the 1948 and 2016 *Rotunda* are listed on page 7.

## Cost of Attending SMU

Every higher learning institution in the United States today has its good and bad attributes, and this certainly applies to Southern Methodist University. SMU offers an excellent college education in many areas of study. SMU's tuition is approximately $43,000 per year, the highest college tuition in the state of Texas.

Breakdowns of some of the 1947 student costs per semester compared to 2015 costs per semester are listed on page 8. There was an 8,418% increase over a seventy-year period.

| SMU Intercollegiate Sports Pages in the *Rotundas* | | |
| --- | --- | --- |
| Sport | 2016 | 1947 |
| Football | 5 | 28 |
| Volleyball | 2 | 0 |
| Women's Basketball | 2 | 0 |
| Men's Basketball | 2 | 12 |
| Golf (Men and Women) | 2 | 0 |
| Women's Soccer | 2 | 0 |
| Men's Soccer | 2 | 0 |
| Women's Swimming and Diving | 2 | 0 |
| Men's Swimming and Diving | 2 | 1 |
| Cross Country | 2 | 0 |
| Track and Field (Women) | 2 | 0 |
| Tennis (Men and Women) | 2 | 1 |
| Equestrian | 2 | 0 |
| Rowing | 2 | 0 |
| Cheer & Pom | 4 | 1 |

Several interesting financial costs in 1947 included:
- The *Rotunda* was part of the student activity fees
- The total cost of textbooks for the year was $15-30
- Married students could live in trailers for $20-27 per month
- If a student went into military service, any unused tuition was refunded pro rata

## Ads in the *Rotundas*

While taking marketing classes in the 1960s at SMU, I learned that not only is advertising a powerful tool for driving sales but also it a reflection of the values of the culture. A list of some advertisers in the 1948 and 2016 *Rotundas* can be found on page 9.

Through the years, advertisements in the *SMU Campus* newspaper have not been as numerous as ads in the *SMU Rotunda*. The 1947 *SMU Campus* ads focused on personal services for the

| SMU Student Costs per Semester | |
|---|---|
| **1947 Costs** | |
| Tuition | $150.00 |
| Board | 150.00 |
| On-campus Housing | 67.50 |
| Student Activity Fee | 11.50 |
| Total | $379.00 |
| **2015 Costs** | |
| Tuition | $21,385 |
| Room and Board | 7,788 |
| Books and Supplies | 400 |
| Other Fees | 2,710 |
| Total | $32,283 |

students and products than 2016 *SMU Campus* ads. Products advertised in 1947 covered a wide range, from Van Heusen shirts to 7 Up soda to shoes from Bridges Shoe Stores. The biggest advertisers in the 1947 *SMU Campus* were big-name cigarette brands, such as Camels or Chesterfield, and the ads were almost always a full page. Famous celebrities, including Rita Hayworth, the Andrews Sisters, Sid Luckman, Ted Williams, and my favorite spokesperson Yankee Clipper Joe DiMaggio, helped promote the specific brands. DiMaggio's line was "Here's the one I'm glad to put my name on… They satisfy me."

## SMU in the 21st Century

In 2015, SMU marked its one-hundredth year. The undergraduate student body of this small, private university has grown to approximately 6,500 students, which is small compared to student bodies of other North Texas public universities that have 40,000 to 50,000 undergraduate students. Academically, SMU always has been ranked as a good school, but not a great school. SMU is not the Harvard of the South or the Rice of the North.

| Advertisers Listed in the *Rotundas* ||
| --- | --- |
| 1948 | 2016 |
| Texas Power & Light Company | Mi Cocina Restaurants |
| Wyatt Food Stores | Fluor Corporation |
| Cullum & Boren Sporting Goods | Verizon Wireless |
| University Drugs | Central Market |
| Humble Oil & Refining Company | Park Place Motors |
| Pig Stands Restaurants | Thompson & Knight, Attorneys |
| Hillcrest State Bank | Ozona Restaurant |
| Metzger's Milk | Preston Road Pharmacy |
| Louann's – Dine and Dance | Ebby Halliday Realtors |

The University has tried to play down its "party school image," but so many beautiful women and handsome men on the Hilltop has made it hard to change this image. Forever imprinted on my mind was my first breakfast on the SMU campus at the student cafeteria in the Umphrey Lee Student Center. In my short nineteen years of life, I had never seen so many gorgeous women who bordered on being "10s" in one room. And this was at 7:00 a.m. before attending class. On his eighty-fifth birthday, Darrel Lindley, who attended SMU in the 1940s, still commented about the number of beautiful SMU co-eds when he attended SMU in 1947.

However today, the prevalence of student alcohol and drug abuse on college campuses is substantial. Recently, the Lambda Chi Alpha fraternity at SMU was suspended from campus for five years by Lambda Chi's National Office. Allegations against the fraternity included the hazing of pledges and fights with other rival SMU fraternities, with both fraternities using baseball bats. In addition, a hard drug ring serving both Lambda Chi brothers and the general student body was being run out of the fraternity house. And finally, one esteemed fraternity member beat his girlfriend to the point of hospitalization. As an SMU business professor in the late 1960s told his Theory of Business Management class, "You men have a lot going for you. You come from good families, your parents make a good income, most of you have a fair amount of intelligence, and some of you even have average looks, but…. you have no soul."

The current SMU President, R. Gerald Turner, is one of the best college fundraisers in the country. President Turner's salary is more than $3 million a year, which makes him one of the top five highest-paid private university presidents in the country. Although a private university can pay its president what it wants, I attended one SMU Student Senate meeting and the Student Senators openly questioned the allocation of their tuition dollars.

When comparing SMU student life after World War II to student life in the early 1960s, the differences are stark. But the differences are even more profound when comparing student life and culture in the 1960s to the culture in the 21st century.

# Chapter Two
# 1947 College Football Season

*"I seen that them men had got into two little bitty bunches down there, they had, real close together and they voted. They did. They voted and elected one man apiece. And them two men came out in the middle of that cow pasture and shook hands like they hadn't seen one another in a long time. And then a convict came over to where they were standing. And he took out a quarter, and they commenced to odd man right there. They did. Well, after a while I'd seen what it was that they were odd-manning for. I seen that both bunches of these men wanted was a funny looking pumpkin to play with. They did. And I know they couldn't eat it because they kicked it all evening and it never busted... Both bunches wanted that thing, and one bunch got it, and it made the other bunch just us mad as they could be. And friends, I'd seen the most awful fight I'd ever seen in my life. I did. They would run at one another and kick one another and thrown one another down. And stomp on one another, and grind their feet in one another. And just as fast as one of them would get hurt they would tote him off and run another one on."*
What It Was, Was Football – Andy Griffith, 1953

The 1947 college football season had three undefeated, untied teams at the end of the regular season. These three teams were Notre Dame, Michigan, and Penn State. At the end of the 1947 bowl games, only Notre Dame (9-0) and Michigan (10-0) were undefeated and untied. The top twenty teams and their records in the final 1947 Associated Press Poll are listed on page 13.

Even with two ties, SMU finished ahead of two undefeated teams — Penn State (which they tied in the Cotton Bowl) and Penn (which only won seven games). Penn State and Penn did not play each other in the 1947 football season.

## Length of Regular Season and Bowl Games

The length of a regular college football schedule varied during the late 1940s. The playing season was usually early September to

late November. If a team was invited to play in a bowl game, it would play at least one more game after the first of the year. The college teams in the 1940s had the discretion to set their schedules so they could play ten games, but that could vary by plus or minus two games. There were thirteen bowl games for the 1947 season, with twelve of these games played on Thursday, January 1, 1948. The Great Lake Bowl was played on Saturday, December 6, 1947, in Cleveland, Ohio. A listing of the thirteen 1947 season bowl games and the results of the bowl games is on page 14.

Nine of the top twenty teams in the final Associated Press poll did not even play in a bowl game in the 1947 postseason bowls. Notre Dame, which had a custom of not playing in bowl games, did not play in a bowl following a perfect 9-0 season. The Fighting Irish not only were undefeated in 1947 but also beat then #9 Army 27-7 in the last game of the season. The Irish also defeated then #3 USC by a score of 38-7 on December 6, 1947. In addition, the 1947 Heisman Trophy winner, Johnny Lujack, was the Irish quarterback during their undefeated season. The following received the top four votes for the 1947 Heisman Trophy:

- Johnny Lujack, Notre Dame (742 votes)
- Bob Chappus, Michigan (555 votes)

- Doak Walker, SMU (196 votes)
- Bobby Layne, Texas (74 votes)

A sports controversy, even fifty years later, was the fact that #1 Notre Dame and #2 Michigan were so even as teams that it was literary a coin toss as to which should be #1 or #2. Notre Dame claimed that the Irish were boycotted by the Big Ten football teams because no Big Ten team would play them. One sports columnist noted in 1947 that the "hottest argument of the moment is the one

| 1947 Associated Press Poll | | |
|---|---|---|
| Ranking | Team | Record |
| 1 | Notre Dame | 9-0-0 |
| 2 | Michigan | 10-0-0 |
| 3 | SMU | 9-0-2 |
| 4 | Penn State | 10-0-1 |
| 5 | Texas | 10-1-0 |
| 6 | Alabama | 8-3-0 |
| 7 | Penn | 7-0-1 |
| 8 | USC | 7-2-1 |
| 9 | North Carolina | 8-2-0 |
| 10 | Georgia Tech | 10-1-0 |
| 11 | Army | 5-2-2 |
| 12 | Kansas | 8-1-2 |
| 13 | Mississippi | 9-2-0 |
| 14 | William & Mary | 9-2-0 |
| 15 | California | 9-1-0 |
| 16 | Oklahoma | 7-2-1 |
| 17 | NC State | 5-3-1 |
| 18 | Rice | 6-3-1 |
| 19 | Duke | 4-3-2 |
| 20 | Columbia | 7-2-0 |

| 1947 Associated Press Poll ||||| 
|---|---|---|---|---|
| Date | Bowl | Teams | Score | Location |
| 1/1/48 | Cotton Bowl | #4 Penn State (10-0-1)<br>#3 SMU (9-0-2) | 13<br>13 | Dallas, TX |
| 1/1/48 | Delta Bowl | #13 Mississippi (9-2)<br>TCU (4-5-2) | 13<br>9 | Memphis, TN |
| 1/1/48 | Dixie Bowl | Arkansas (6-4-1)<br>#14 William & Mary (9-2) | 21<br>19 | Birmingham, AL |
| 1/1/48 | Gator Bowl | Maryland (10-2-1)<br>Georgia (7-4-1) | 20<br>20 | Jacksonville, FL |
| 1/1/48 | Harbor Bowl | Hardin-Simmons (10-2)<br>San Diego State (10-2) | 53<br>0 | San Diego, CA |
| 1/1/48 | Orange Bowl | #10 Georgia Tech (10-1)<br>#12 Kansas (8-1-2) | 20<br>14 | Miami, FL |
| 1/1/48 | Raisin Bowl | Pacific (10-2)<br>Wichita State (7-4) | 26<br>14 | Fresno, CA |
| 1/1/48 | Rose Bowl | #2 Michigan (10-0)<br>#8 Southern Cal (7-2-1) | 49<br>0 | Pasadena, CA |
| 1/1/48 | Salad Bowl | Nevada (10-2)<br>North Texas (10-2) | 13<br>6 | Phoenix, AZ |
| 1/1/48 | Sugar Bowl | #5 Texas (10-1)<br>#6 Alabama (8-3) | 27<br>7 | New Orleans, LA |
| 1/1/48 | Sun Bowl | Miami-OH (7-3)<br>Texas Tech (6-5) | 13<br>12 | El Paso, TX |
| 1/1/48 | Tangerine Bowl | Catawba College (11-1)<br>Marshall (9-3) | 7<br>0 | Orlando, FL |
| 12/6/47 | Great Lakes Bowl | Kentucky (8-3)<br>Villanova (6-3-1) | 24<br>14 | Cleveland, OH |

over which had the better football team, Michigan or Notre Dame." To help settle the matter the Associated Press polled more than 350 sports writers in 48 states and the vote was two to one for the Wolverines. Despite this, the Fighting Irish were named the No. 1 team in the final Associated Press poll.

## Eligibility to a Bowl Game

In 1947, each bowl committee or a city's selection committee chose the teams for their bowl game. Most bowls matched teams that either were ranked in the top twenty or were not ranked at all. It is interesting to note that even though the TCU Horned Frogs had a 4-4-2 regular season record, they played in the Delta Bowl. The Frogs lost to #13 Mississippi 13-9 in the game played in Memphis, Tennessee.

During the 1947 season, many teams ended with tie scores. Of the top twenty teams, ten teams had one or more ties, and four teams had two tie games. It should be noted that in 1947, the offensives and defenses of college football teams were more balanced than today's teams. In fact, there were even six 0-0 ties during the 1947 season, between Kansas-TCU, Dartmouth-Holy Cross, Illinois-Army, South Carolina-Duke, George Washington-Georgetown, and Maryland-North Carolina State.

An interesting side note was that until 1949, there was no restriction as to the number of bowl games a college football team could play after the regular season ended. The Hardin-Simmons Cowboys played in three bowl games from December 9 to December 30, 1948, after the close of the regular 1948 season. They posted a 2-1 record in their bowl games. The next year the NCAA passed a rule limiting college teams to one bowl appearance per year. This rule was changed in 2015 to allow for the current college football playoff system in which four teams qualify and two teams play two playoff games.

The current Division I bowl eligibility rules fill approximately a page and a half of small print on the NCAA website. The ruling didn't seem to slow down a record forty bowl games for the 2015 season, and three 2015 college teams played in bowls even though they had losing records (5-7 San Jose State, 5-7 Minnesota, and 5-7 Nebraska).

## Size of Football Squads and Coaching Staffs

In the 1940s, the size of varsity college football squads was approximately half the size of today's college football squads. The 1947 SMU team had approximately 46 players, but the 2015 SMU team listed 133 players. The main reason for the increased number of players is that freshman now are eligible to play on varsity squads, whereas in the 1940s, freshman players only played on freshman or B-team squads at the collegiate level. Also in 2015, the NCAA has rules regarding the number of years a player can play, which includes red-shirting and school transferring, both of which affect squad size. However, the biggest change over the 68-year period is the size of the coaching staff. Although pictures of the 1947 squad included six coaches, 1947 player John Hamberger said only three coaches coached the 1947 SMU squad on a daily basis. These coaches were head coach Matty Bell, Rusty Russell, who worked with backs, and line coach McAdoo Kenton.

The 2015 coaching staff was much more specialized, with head coach Chad Morris and ten coaches who had direct position responsibilities. Also, nineteen individuals were involved with the football team and had duties that ranged from equipment manager to director of video productions.

## Freshman Eligibility

During the World War II years, some schools allowed freshman to play on varsity teams, so in the early 1940s, there was no NCAA rule on freshman play. Colleges and universities had the discretion to set player eligibility. During the war years, many smaller colleges dropped football entirely because of a lack of players. If World War II had gone on for another three to four years (if the atomic bombs had not ended the war), many of the players who played college football in the late 1940s never would have come back from the Pacific theater. If World War II had continued to the late 1940s, SMU's special football year of 1947 probably never would have happened.

Many freshman players played fewer games their freshman, year as most B-team schedules were only five or six games. However, the 1946 SMU B-team played a ten-game season and finished with an 8-1-1 record. Also, no player on the 1946 SMU B-team was a starter on the 1947 SMU varsity team. In the 1940s, B-team games in the Southwest Conference usually were against other Southwest Conference B-teams. B-team squads could scrimmage varsity squads and most likely run the same offense and defense formations as the varsity team.

In 1972, freshmen on all NCAA football teams were eligible for varsity play. Today, however, some conference commissioners are considering freshman ineligibility in their conferences. The commissioners primarily have targeted college basketball freshman to discourage college basketball players from playing one-and-done seasons before going to play in professional basketball. There is a low probability that freshman ineligibility would be for all male freshman playing college football and basketball. The decision primarily depends on new player eligibility rules that might come from both the NBA and the NFL.

## Players Played Both Ways

The biggest difference in college football in 1947 and 2015 was that in 1947 most starters played both offense and defense. A starting player was a true sixty-minute player. Many teams even had a starter, like Doak Walker, who also was a kicker. My biggest joy from playing organized football was playing both offense and defense in a B-team game against the Corpus Christi Roy Miller Buccaneers in the early 1960s. It was like playing a different game, and it was a football high that I can never forget. If you could compare two-platoon college football to another major sport like baseball, it would be like one unit only batting and one unit is only fielding. Now, how dumb would that be? As a two-way football player, you never left the field except for an occasional substitution.

Unlimited substitution became more common in college football until 1953, when the NCAA established rules that enforced one-platoon football. Tennessee head football coach Robert Neyland praised the change as the end of "chickenshit football." However, eleven years later in 1964, the NCAA reversed the one-platoon rule, and two-platoon college football was here to stay.

Some of the greatest football players in American football were one-platoon players. Most of these players, including Jim Thorpe, Red Grange, Don Hutson, Chuck Bednarik, and Slinging Sammy Baugh, also played one-platoon football in the NFL. Bednarik was an outspoken critic of the two-platoon system. He was also the last player to play both ways in an NFL championship game when playing for the Philadelphia Eagles in 1960.

## Total Time of Game

The total playing time for college football games always has been sixty minutes. However, sixty minutes of actual playing time in today's college football can take as much as four hours to play. It appears that baseball is the only sport in America concerned with the total time it takes to play a game. Even with the current speed-up passing offenses of today's college football games, some SMU football quarters can take as much as an hour to play. If the average SMU fan today decides to go to the Boulevard before an SMU game, that fan could experience a six- to seven-hour game day experience.

For the 2015 SMU football player, the longer total game time means lengthy time of doing nothing but standing on the field or on the sidelines. The two major consumers of time are TV timeouts and lengthy reviews of plays that, to the fans in the stands, seem to be reviewed for no apparent reason.

## Offensive and Defensive Formations

Since most of the players played both ways in the 1947 season, the emphasis was on the offensive side of the ball. Practice time was at a premium, so the concentration of time was on how a team could score. John Hamberger said the 1947 SMU team had only three defensive formations and spent a little time practicing defensive formations. In addition, Hamberger said that one of the defensive formations was the "goal-line stand," which probably didn't require much team practice.

In 1947, the two major offensive formations were the single-wing formation and the T formation. The single-wing formation was developed by Glenn "Pop" Warner when he coached the Carlisle Indians in 1907. The single wing is probably the only offensive football formation designed solely around the ability of one football player. Pop Warner's outstanding player at Carlisle was Jim Thorpe, a Native American who many sports analysts consider the greatest American athlete of all time. Like Doak Walker, Thorpe could do it all on a football field – pass, run, receive, kick, and punt. The single-wing offense was brought to SMU by 1947 assistant coach Rusty Russell for the sole purpose of capitalizing on the football talents of Doak Walker.

Carl "The Grey Fox" Snavely, who coached college football for 37 years, won a national championship at Cornell in 1939, and is in the College Football Hall of Fame once said, "There is no way to improve on football beyond the unbalanced line single-wing." The single-wing formation is unique because of the many variations that can be executed from the basic formation. The single-line can execute with either a balanced or unbalanced line. Knute Rockne developed several variations of the single-wing using a balanced line. The flexing of offensive ends, the shifting of the backfield, the double-wing variation, and the use of a "spinner" back who could spin as much as 360 degrees in handing off the football all were variations of the single-wing that were made to confuse the defense.

## Looking Back

In 1947, college football only somewhat resembled college football of 2015. Many aspects of 1947 college football were closer to 2015 American rugby football than 2015 college football.

Although the 1947 college football season was vastly different from today's college football, some things have remained the same. Every season there is usually a controversy over which Division I team is rated No. 1. Even with "instant replay," there are controversies over certain plays or final scores. Fans argue over who might be the best college player in a certain year, and why their school needs to fire their coach and hire a coach who can take their team at least to a conference championship.

But college football still comes down to what Andy Griffith described as the most awful fight he'd ever seen in his life. "They would run at one another and kick one another and throw one another down. And stomp on one another, and grind their feet in one another." Because whether the year is 1947 or 2015, the sport is still American college football.

# Chapter Three
# Ewell Doak Walker, Jr.

## Saying Goodbye to Doak Walker

*"He's Doak Walker, and he was as golden as golden gets. He had perfectly even white teeth and a jaw as square as a deck of cards and a mop of brown hair that made girls bite their necklaces. He was so shifty you couldn't have tackled him in a phone booth, yet so humble that he wrote the Associated Press a thank-you note for naming him an All-American. Come to think of it, he was a three-time All-American, twice one of the Outstanding Players in the Cotton Bowl, a four-time All-Pro. He appeared on forty-seven covers, including Life, Look, and Collier's. One time, Kyle Rote, another gridiron golden boy, saw a guy buying a football magazine at a newsstand. 'Don't buy that one,' Rote said. 'It's not official. It doesn't have a picture of Doak Walker on the cover.'"*

Having played some football in Texas in elementary, junior high, high school, and college, I was always aware, as a player, of a team's need for that special player. Even though coaches emphasize that football is a team sport, players always know that just one outstanding player could and would make a huge difference on a team, especially if that special player could touch the ball playing at a so-called "skill position." Playing in a high school B-squad game in 1961 in Alice, Texas, I thought if only our quarterback Bill Whitaker was just a little better passer, we could easily have beaten an inferior and less skilled Alice Coyote team.

The SMU team of 1946 was mediocre at best, with a 4-5-1 record. The University of Arkansas and Rice University were co-champions of the Southwest Conference in 1946, and the University of Texas and Rice University were the odds-on favorites to win the Southwest Conference in 1947. Players always hoped that they not only would get that "special player" when they were playing, but also that the player would not get injured or drop out of school.

In 1947, the SMU football team not only got a "special player," they got a player who many consider being the greatest college

*Ewell Doak Walker, Jr.*

football player of all time. Although he was not the perfect football player, Ewell Doak Walker Jr. came close and is considered a once in a hundred-year player. In Walker's two prime years at SMU, the team went 18-1-3. During his senior year in 1949, Walker was plagued with injuries and was even in street clothes for the highly anticipated SMU/Notre Dame game that year. After the Doak Walker era, SMU didn't win another Southwest Conference championship until 1966, when a Hayden Fry team went 8-3-0 and played Georgia in the Cotton Bowl, losing 24-9.

## Growing Up in Dallas

Born in Dallas, Texas, on January 1, 1927, Doak Walker grew up in Highland Park, where he excelled in sports at an early age. He received a football for his second birthday. By the time he was in kindergarten, he could drop-kick the ball over the backyard clothesline. His father Doak Sr. said, "He was such a little tyke that I told him that anyone who could kick could make the team." When he was in the fourth grade, he was playing in full pads with sixth graders at University Park Grade School. In high school, he lettered in football (four years), basketball (three years), swimming (three years), baseball (two years), and track. Also In high school, Walker acquired the nickname, "Robin, the Wonder Boy." Beginning in high school, he also started to attract the Highland Park girls. For three summers, Doak was a lifeguard at the University Park pool, where he was the idol of more than one bobbysoxer. During his senior year of high school in 1944, Walker was named All-State and All-Southern in football. After his freshman year at SMU, Walker was drafted and served in the Merchant Marines and the Army for about fourteen months. His only comment regarding his military experience was that it was "a good place with nothing to do and lots of time to do it in."

One of the biggest moments in SMU football history occurred when Walker got out of the Army and was ready to play college football. It was October 27, 1945. Walker was in New Orleans with Bobby Layne, his best friend in high school, to attend an SMU/Tulane football game. Layne had graduated from high school a year before Walker and had made a commitment to the University of Texas. Layne was taking Walker to see Blair Cherry, the Texas football head coach, to confirm an oral commitment Walker had made to attend Texas. As Walker and Layne were taking an elevator up to Cherry's hotel room, Cherry was taking an elevator down to check out of the hotel. It was a missed connection. If Walker and Cherry had met that day, Doak Walker probably would have worn burnt orange instead of SMU's red and blue.

## SMU Football Experience

In 1947, the sophomore Walker was slight of build, weighing in at 170 pounds and 5' 11" in height. The 1947 season was the first year that Walker played on the varsity squad and was his first year to be named an All-American. In the Heisman Trophy balloting, Walker finished a distant third to Johnny Lujack of Notre Dame. Lujack received 742 votes, Bob Chappus of Michigan received 555 votes, and Walker finished third with 196 votes. Ironically, the Heisman voting followed the final rankings of the 1947 football teams, with Notre Dame first, Michigan second, and SMU third. Walker was an All-American all three of his varsity SMU years. Walker also won the Maxwell Award in 1947 and the Heisman Award in 1948 as a junior.

Sixty years later, Joe Redwine Patterson told the story that one day on the SMU campus a magazine reporter asked him to point out Doak Walker, who was walking near Dallas Hall. When Patterson did identify Walker, the reporter couldn't believe that the average-looking, short, bumbling kid was "the Doak Walker." However, Walker was more highly regarded by his SMU head football coach, Matty Bell, who said of Walker, "Some called it luck, others called it destiny. But Doak had a natural knack for pulling off great deeds. He was the ideal player and the ideal boy. Nobody ever played football like Doak Walker."

Walker's legacy at SMU and college football far surpassed anything else he did in life. His accomplishments on the football field deeply affected both Dallas and SMU. The Cotton Bowl was nicknamed "The House that Doak Built" because of its expansion to a second deck when Doak arrived in 1947. The Cotton Bowl was not exactly "the House that Doak Built," but more accurately it was "The House that Doak Doubled." The Cotton Bowl capacity doubled from 45,000 to 72,000. In addition, the "Doak Walker Award" is awarded annually to the best running back in college football. I have always thought the best running back award should have been named after a pure running back like Eric Dickerson, rather than Walker. Walker did far more than just run with a football, as he passed as much as ran in SMU's single wing formation.

There are a couple of busts of individuals as well as a statue of the first Peruna at the miniature horse's gravesite. In addition, there is a statue of three Mustangs in front of Moody Coliseum that depicts nameless mustang horses running in different directions. But the one statue of an SMU alumnus — Doak Walker — is located on the northeast corner of Gerald Ford Stadium. Walker is in his full SMU football uniform with a football tucked under his right arm, and his football helmet appears to be too big for his head. One leg extends off the ground and one arm is outstretched to stiff-arm would-be tacklers. Walker is depicted running, with his eyes focused in the direction of the site of the former Ownby Stadium. Statues of individuals, especially generals at war, sometimes are erected at the site of their greatest triumph. However, Walker only played two SMU varsity football games in Ownby Stadium. All his other home SMU games were in the Cotton Bowl. With SMU playing in the Cotton Bowl, large crowds from Dallas and the surrounding North Texas area could see the little kid from Highland Park work his magic on the football field. The Doak Walker statue was dedicated on October 27, 2001, fifty-six years to the day after Walker and Cherry failed to meet in a New Orleans hotel.

The SMU football seasons of 1947-1948 were Walker's two magical seasons. Many college football fans, still consider these seasons the two best seasons of any player in the history of college football. Unfortunately, injuries and illness plagued Walker's senior year of football in 1949. In thirty-five college football games, Walker gained 2.2 miles net rushing and passing and was also named the Top Male Athlete of Dallas' first 100 years.

## Friendship of Paul Page

In the 1947 season, Walker also developed a deep personal relationship with fellow backfield player Paul Page. The two teammates had a lifelong friendship based on mutual values, humility, and conservative Christian values. In a letter to one of the Page's children in 1997, shortly after Page's death, Walker wrote about his friend Paul," He touched so many persons during his whole life. I'm very proud to say I was a friend."

## Football Honors

Walker's performance playing high school and college football in Texas earned him many honors, including induction into the Texas Sports Hall of Fame in 1959, the Texas High School Football Hall of Fame in 1973, and the Southwest Conference Hall of Fame in 2013. However, one of his highest honors came from Grantland

Rice, who once called Doak Walker "the most authentic all-around player in football history."

## Football Career after SMU

Walker was drafted in the 1949 NFL draft as the No. 3 pick by the Boston Yanks. The Detroit Lions acquired his draft rights in 1950, and he played through six NFL seasons (1950-1955). He was all-pro for four years and helped the Lions win back-to-back world championships in 1952 and 1953. Walker was the leading scorer of the NFL his final year of pro-football, but at the age of twenty-eight, he suddenly retired. When asked why he retired so young, he said, "If I could have played pro football the rest of my life I would have, but I couldn't play forever, so I got out. I didn't want to be one of those guys who played one season too long." The football legend had become football history. Walker's induction into the Pro Football Hall of Fame in 1986 was thirty-one years after his last pro football game. Most of Walker's scoring in pro football was field goals and extra points (330 points out of 534 points scored). Over the years, sports analysts have debated Walker's merit as a pro football player and whether he deserves the honors he received in playing pro football. However, as early as the mid-1950s, the pro football careers of smaller and lighter players were beginning to close.

## Life Goes On

If Walker was close to Mr. Perfect, he dated an equally noted sweetheart while attending SMU. Norma Peterson was a *Rotunda* beauty and sorority girl who was featured prominently in both the *SMU Campus* and the *Rotunda* in 1947 and 1948. Walker and Peterson appeared in several ads on the *SMU Campus* even after they had graduated SMU. One *SMU Campus* ad promoted Arthur Everts Jewelers with a picture of the happy couple selecting china and silver at the so-called "Fifth Quarter 1950 Football Party." Peterson and Walker married at the Highland Park Presbyterian Church on March 17, 1950. They had four children together, but the marriage lasted only until 1967.

Walker left Dallas for good in 1957 and had no desire to return. Although he made a few visits back over the years, his visits only included being introduced during half-time at SMU home football games. He often said that Dallas had become "a phony town." He worked for many years in Denver as vice president of corporate sales for a national electrical and mechanical contractor. In 1969, he married Skeeter Warner, a former American ski champion.

## The End

Doak Walker died on September 27, 1998, as a result of complications from a ski accident that had occurred eight months earlier in Colorado. A service was at Highland Park Presbyterian Church, the same church at which he married his college sweetheart forty-eight years earlier. Dr. Clayton Bell officiated the service, and Rod Hanna, Bill Lively, and Verne Lundquist offered words of remembrance. The only direct connection to SMU during the service was music played by the SMU Band. At the service, it was announced that the October 17 SMU/TCU game would be Doak Walker Game Day; Walker was always ready to play against TCU.

# Chapter Four
# Madison A. Bell

*"We haven't got a chance. My backs are all crippled up, and my line would look better if they were sick. The way they have been playing makes me sick, and Texas outweighs us two tons to a man. They have big fast boys while all we got is little-undernourished students; I hope we can hold the score down to where there will be enough fans in the stands to watch our band between halves." Morris Frank is mimicking Matty Bell.*

## The "Great White Father" of SMU Sports

Madison A. Bell provided the stabling influence and the coaching experience that pushed the 1947 team to reach its season's goal of going to the Cotton Bowl. Bell had a head coaching background and was familiar with Texas college football, having coached both at TCU (1923-1928) and Texas A&M (1929-1933). Bell played high school football at Northside High School in Fort Worth. In 1915, Bell's senior year at Northside, the team won, by some accounts, the Texas high school football championship. After the championship season, Centre College in Danville, Kentucky, recruited Northside coach Robert "Chief" Meyers as an assistant coach and four of the senior players. Meyers became head coach at Centre College in the 1925 and 1926 seasons.

Matty Bell played multiple positions at Centre College, including quarter, center, guard, tackle, and end. Bell lettered in football in 1916-1919 and in basketball in 1917-1920. Bell was captain of the football team his senior year and was named an All-Kentucky end that same year.

The Praying Colonels were a college football powerhouse during Bell's playing years at Centre College. In the 1917 season, the Colonels went 8-1, and despite losing to Kentucky 68-0, they only allowed a single touchdown the remainder of the season. The Old Centre Yearbook noted that Bell made a spectacular touchdown run of 65 yards against Georgetown in the last game of the 1917 season. In 1918, the Colonels outscored their opposition 279-7. The 1919 season was even more impressive, as the Praying Colonels posted an 8-0 record while outscoring their opposition 512-22. The team avenged its 1918 loss to DePauw by beating DePauw 56-0 and Hanover 95-0. Centre College's overall record when Bell was playing was 25-2-3.

The character of Matty Bell was reflected in the Centre College yearbooks when he was a student. Bell went by the nicknames of "Skeet" and "Long Goody." A write-up on Bell in the 1920 Old Centre yearbook reflected his character "Skeet is one of our best-loved Texas steers. He is an athlete of many attainments and a gentleman with many friends."

The Centre College football juggernaut ran from 1915 through the mid-1920s. The hot recruiting area for Centre College was in

Ft. Worth, Texas, because of many blue-collar workers who worked in the Fort Worth Stockyards and had athletic sons. From 1917 to 1929, Centre College had a record of fifty-seven wins and eight losses. The 1921 team was undefeated and outscored its opponents 314-6.

The Praying Colonels' most noted football game in the school's history was their 6-0 upset of Harvard before 40,000 fans at Harvard Stadium in 1921. Many in the sports press have called the 1921 Harvard-Centre College game the greatest upset in American college football history as well as the greatest upset in the history of American sports. The Harvard-Centre College game is well documented in Robert Robertson's excellent book "The Wonder Team – The Story of the Centre College Praying Colonels and their Rise to the Top of the Football World 1917-1924."

Of even more importance to Texas A&M fans is its game against Centre College in the 1922 Dixie Classic Bowl game. At the time, Centre College was college football's defending national champion. The Dixie Classic Bowl was Centre College's second bowl game of the season; the Colonels already had defeated Arizona 38-0 in the East-West Christmas Classic on December 26. As the Aggies' injuries mounted in the Dixie Classic Bowl on January 2, they turned to the stands to find a replacement player for the injured squad. Even though the substitute A&M player never entered the game, this was the beginning of one of the most famous American college football traditions — the Texas A&M 12th Man.

During his entire coaching career, Bell was only an assistant football coach one year, which was unique for a college football coach. Bell was the line coach at SMU in 1934. Bell's first head coaching job was at Haskell Institute, in Lawrence, Kansas, where he was the head coach of the Fighting Indians. Not only was the team name the Fighting Indians, but the team members were true Native American Indians. Coaches could play with their football teams at Haskell Institute, so Bell played with the Indian squad. Since he did not have the same physique as the student players, he earned the nickname, "Hiawatha."

When head coach Ray Morrison left SMU to become head football coach at Vanderbilt University, Bell was promoted from line coach and became SMU's head football coach in 1935. In his

*Matty Bell and Dutch Meyer*
*Two unlikely looking college head football coaches by today's standards*

first year as SMU's head coach, SMU won the school's only College Football National Championship. Bell coached the SMU team to a 12-0-0 regular season record before losing to Stanford in the Rose Bowl 7-0. Bell coached at SMU from 1934 through 1949, with a break from 1942 to 1945, when he served in the Navy and coached physical fitness to World War II Navy recruits in Athens, Georgia.

Bell's overall coaching record at SMU was seventy-nine wins, forty losses, and eight ties. Bell ranks as the second most winning

SMU Coaches talk it over before 1948 Cotton Bowl

SMU coach in the history of SMU football. Bell's record at TCU was thirty-three wins, seventeen losses, and five ties. His football record at Texas A&M was twenty-four wins, twenty-one losses, and three ties. Bell's overall college football record was 143-87-16, and he entered the College Football Hall of Fame in 1955. The only other SMU head football coach to be inducted into the College Football Hall of Fame is Hayden Fry. After the 1949 football season, Bell served as SMU's Director of Athletics until 1964. Among Bell's accomplishments as SMU Athletic Director are five Southwest Conference basketball championships, the 1956 opening of Moody Coliseum, ten Southwest Conference men's swimming and diving championships, and SMU's only NCAA golf championship in 1954.

Bell has other connections to TCU, SMU's biggest rival. In addition to coaching the Frog football team, Bell also coached the TCU basketball team from 1923 to 1929 and recorded a 71-41 record. He also hired Dutch Meyer as the TCU freshman football coach in 1923. Meyer coached football at TCU for nineteen years and led the team to its only NCAA football national championship in 1938. Meyer also is noted for his football innovations in S. C.

*Matty Bell was also a great father to daughter Patty*

Gwynne's book the "Perfect Pass." Meyer used the "shotgun" formation in the 1930s with Sammy Baugh. Gwynne wrote, "The double wing 'Meyer spread' was devastating and produced unprecedented passing yardage."

Bell is the only SMU head football coach to be honored with an appreciation dinner. On November 6, 1970, approximately 250 guests attended the event at the Umphrey Lee Student Union building on the SMU campus. The appreciation dinner highlighted Bell's infamous tagline "The Great White Father." Most of the 1947 football squad probably didn't need "a father image" after serving in World War II. However, the football team did need the same discipline on the football field that the many World War II veteran football players had when they were in the military. Bell gave them that discipline, but he also gave them more. As Walker said at the Bell appreciation dinner, "He (Matty) would tell us: It's only sixty minutes on the field, but there'll be a lifetime to remember it."

When Bell died at the age of 84 on June 30, 1983, an article in *The Dallas Morning News*, "Glory on the Hilltop", commented on his passing. Bell's character was shown through his support and attendance at the Salesmanship Club Camp at Buchman Lake in Dallas. He wanted to show he cared about troubled Dallas kids. Even though Bell was a tough disciplinarian, his players all knew

Matty Bell welcomed Haden Fry to the Hilltop in 1962. Fry and Bell are the only two SMU Head Coaches to be in the NCAA Football Hall of Fame.

he cared. From a group of American Indians at a small college in Kansas to a group of World War II veterans playing at SMU, Matty Bell earned his unofficial title of the "Great White Father."

Bell continued to receive honors for his coaching long after his coaching days. Inductions into the Texas Sports Hall of Fame in 1960 and the Southwest Conference Hall of Fame in 2013 were just two of his many honors.

During Bell's time at SMU, the university had a college football national champion, a Heisman Trophy winner, All-Americans, an undefeated season, and back-to-back Cotton Bowl appearances, as well as SMU's only time to play in the Rose Bowl. Bell's coaching accolades at SMU more than likely will never be equaled again on the Hilltop.

# Chapter Five
# Joe Redwine Patterson

Joe Redwine Patterson was one of the big personalities at SMU in 1947. However, his love of SMU did not end when he graduated in 1949. Patterson continued to be a strong supporter of SMU football even until his late 80s.

Patterson was the elected head cheerleader for the 1947 football season and president of the SMU student body in 1948. Starting at SMU in 1943, Patterson played varsity football at SMU primarily, as a blocking dummy. Patterson was drafted into the Navy in 1944, had he told me that he was sure he would have died on an isolated beach in Japan if it had not been for the dropping of the atomic bombs on Hiroshima and Nagasaki, Japan. After joining the Navy, he was trained to pilot a Navy landing craft. Patterson thought it odd that the Navy trained all the landing craft personnel on the use of an M-1 rifle. His first thought was, "Why do I need a rifle if I'm in the Navy and never be on land?" To its credit, the U.S. Navy was upfront in telling the first wave sailors and marines that thousands of U.S. troops would not survive that first day of a beach landing on the shores of homeland Japan.

## The First Meeting

I first met Patterson through Tom Kelly, Gamma Sigma #718, who grew up in North Canton, Ohio, but moved to Dallas and attended Thomas Jefferson High School before attending SMU. Kelly graduated from SMU with a government degree and then attended SMU's Law School. After law school, Kelly went to work for the Dallas law firm of Patterson, Lamberty, which later became Patterson, Lamberty, & Kelly. My first encounters with Patterson was going to opening day Texas Ranger baseball games with a group put together by Kelly. Not only did we go to Ranger games together, but the group then would go to Shakey's pizza after the game for pizza and beer. Patterson started the tradition of having the Shakey banjo players play Happy Birthday for Ranger player Rico Carty. Rico "Beeg Boy" Carty was a favorite of the group, but Carty's actual birthday is September 1. I got to know Patterson better over the years by playing handball with Patterson at the Downtown Dallas YMCA. Over a 12-year period, we played 292 handball games, including three games on the last day the old downtown YMCA was open. The date of those last three handball games was January

12, 1982. The downtown YMCA moved to a new facility across the street later that month. A bit of trivia about the old YMCA was that Lee Harvey Oswald had lived there for a brief period when he first moved to Dallas. One of my fondest memories of playing handball with Patterson occurred when he stormed onto the handball court about fifteen minutes late for a singles match. "Damn that judge. (I assumed from his court trial of the day.) Everything is going wrong today. Even these shorts (the gym shorts he was wearing) don't fit right." "That is because you have them on backward," I subtly explained to a frazzled Joe Red.

Patterson was born on April 16, 1927, in Corsicana, Texas. His middle name Redwine was an old family name dating back to the 1800s in Virginia. To many of his fellow students and classmates at SMU, he was simply known as "Redwine" or "Joe Red." Forty years later whenever I met an SMU graduate that I knew attended SMU in the 1940s, I only had to say one word — Redwine — and they could tell me their favorite SMU story about him. In the years after SMU, Redwine was the moniker that most people associated with Patterson. For many years, he had a personalized license plate "Joe Red," which was attached to a beat-up, high-mileage Volvo station wagon.

My best recollection of the Volvo "Joe Red" was seeing the vehicle speeding down Hillcrest Avenue on a Sunday morning at 8:00 a.m. going about 60 mph. Redwine was not at the wheel, but instead, his son Joe Redwine Patterson, Jr. was driving. High school-aged Joe Jr., while puffing on a cigarette, had one hand on the steering wheel and the other arm around a cute blond teenage classmate. (Like father, like son.) However, Redwine was adamantly against smoking, which unfortunately caused a long-time rift with son Joe Jr.

## Growing up in Rural Texas

Joe's father, Rev. Joseph Isham Patterson, was a Methodist minister who graduated from SMU and earned his divinity degree from the SMU's Perkins School of Theology. The Rev. Patterson had played football for SMU during the 1916-1917 seasons. In true Methodist minister tradition, the senior Patterson served mainly small rural Methodist churches west of Fort Worth on a rotating basis. Joe grew up with two strong influences – rural North Texas in the 1930s and 1940s, and the moral values of the Methodist church. Redwine said several times that being the son of a Methodist minister had placed a "lifelong restriction on his moral compass."

Redwine had two brothers, James and Julian. Growing up in a household with three brothers in a rural Texas environment produced some interesting family dynamics for the Patterson family. Joe's recollections of his early childhood years primarily included performing chores, like milking the family cow and having ongoing fist fights with brother Jim. Jim went by the nickname "Jim White," his middle name and his mother's maiden name. The family had a "Jim White" and a "Joe Red." The brotherly fights escalated during high school to the point at which Joe's mother, Caroline, said, "Joe Red, I'm tired of your fighting with your brother Jim White. You need to fight someone else for a change." At a point of high anxiety, Mother Patterson signed Redwine to fight in the high school division of Fort Worth Golden Gloves. Unfortunately, Redwine's first fight was an orphan from the Masonic Home of Fort Worth. As Jim Dent observed in his book, *Twelve Angry Orphans*, there was no child meaner in the State of Texas during the 1930s and 1940s than an orphan from the Masonic Home of Fort Worth. Redwine made it only to the opening bell of the second round. The Golden Gloves fight was Redwine's last official refereed fight. Redwine retired with a record of 0-1 from the boxing ring.

## Times at SMU

Even when Redwine arrived on the SMU campus as a freshman, he was already bleeding red and blue. The SMU colors are from the Harvard red and the Yale blue. Rev. Patterson had taken Redwine on many trips to visit the SMU campus before he enrolled at SMU. Joe knew many of the professors and administrators at SMU by name and had met them on numerous occasions. After his freshman year in 1943, Joe went into the Navy, where he served for almost two years before returning to the campus as a sophomore in 1946.

After serving as head cheerleader in 1947, Redwine was elected SMU student body president in 1948. His term as student body president was a period of what could best be described as "a mighty

*Redwine approaches Peruna with a blanket in front of Dallas Hall*

clash of egos." Another strong personality at SMU in the late 1940s was Aaron Spelling, of later Hollywood producing fame. Spelling was elected head cheerleader in 1948 following Patterson's tenure of 1947. As on many college campuses in the United States, there was a social divide between the Greeks and non-Greeks, and SMU was no exception. Although the student body was a non-Greek majority, almost all the student leaders, including student senators, the homecoming court, and *Rotunda* beauties, were fraternity and sorority students. Aaron Spelling was an SAE, and Joe Patterson was a GDI.

Redwine was part of a spirited campaign to become student body president for the 1948-1949 school year. Five candidates — as reported by the *SMU Campus* of April 28, 1948, Buddy Forbis, Paul Petty, Gilman Grey, Bill Wood, and Joe Redwine Patterson — were campaigning hard for the coveted position. Patterson won on a strong ten-point platform. Even sixty years later, Darryl Lynch of the class of 1949 remembered four of the points in Redwine's ten-point platform. The ten platform points were:
1. Better football seats for SMU students.
2. More tickets available to students.
3. Including instructors' names on class registration schedules.
4. Uniform absence regulations in all departments.

5. Menu improvement in campus dining halls.
6. Use of meal tickets in dining halls.
7. Improved parking situation.
8. A bigger and better SMU campus.
9. Student Council improvement: in spirit and organization.
10. Improved intramural program.

Better SMU football tickets do not mean much to 2015 SMU students. With an improved basketball team, under then head basketball coach Larry Brown, students were told that they would receive more points to get SMU basketball tickets if they attended home SMU football games. Several SMU football players quoted in the *SMU campus* newspaper said they hoped the students wouldn't attend any SMU football games if they were only attending football games so they could get basketball tickets.

## Reprimand of Cheerleaders and Impeachment of Redwine

A major tradition in college football in the 1940s was the campus bonfire. Many colleges had bonfires during football season, particularly before the football game against their biggest rivals. SMU's biggest rival was, and still is, Texas Christian University, which was a member of the Southwest Conference and was located only a short 35 miles away. In the 1930s and early 1940s, TCU was a football powerhouse, and is best described in Dan Jenkin's greatly entertaining and informative article in Sports Illustrated, "They Might be Kings."

Before the 1948 SMU/TCU game, there was the traditional gathering of wood for the SMU bonfire. Central metropolitan Dallas was not a land of abundant wood for a bonfire in the 1940s and is even less so today. Highland Park residents were on high alert before the annual SMU/TCU game for SMU students looking for any piece of wood that was not nailed down, and even some wood that was nailed down. Often, Highland Park residents would wake up to find their wooden fences missing more than a few slats of wood. Spelling's fraternity was among the groups collecting bonfire wood with typical frat enthusiasm.

The Student Senate severely reprimanded Spelling for gathering

*Aaron Spelling*
*One of SMU's Most Famous Alumni*

firewood for the bonfire without the permission of the SMU student government. He countered by bringing impeachment proceedings against Patterson for defamation of his character that would affect his chances of being successful after he graduated from SMU. The case went to the SMU student court and Patterson's tenure as SMU's Student Body President subject to the court's ruling.

## Student Council Reports All Cheerleaders Guilty of Violating Constitution

The December 8 issue of the *SMU Campus* stated the severity of the council's charges against the cheerleaders, "By holding a wood gathering without the consent of the Council, the cheerleader committed to action in direct opposition to the constitution. Holding such a contest and restricting it to only social organizations on campus is both a breach of the Constitution and an affront to the spirit of the Student's Association".

A December 15 *SMU Campus* article titled, "Spelling, Patterson Appear in Court for First Hearing," reported that Spelling followed with a complaint against Patterson. The complaint was "that Patterson and the Council members did unlawfully subject him to reprimand, ridicule, embarrassment, and persecution ..., and asked for a hearing before the Student Court to try the questions of law and fact."

The trial, Spelling vs. Patterson, was probably the biggest non-sporting event on campus in the 1948-1949 school years. A packed room of more than 350 students attended the four-hour trial, hearing testimony that sometimes brought forth laughter and applause from the audience. In addition, chief justice Kirby Ellis constantly reminded the counsels to make their comments less repetitious. Spelling's initial statement from the witness stand was, "Patterson told me he didn't give a damn how I made it, but to make it the biggest bonfire I could for the homecoming game." Patterson denied making that statement. In Patterson's testimony, he stated, "The cheerleaders were told in a meeting November 4 that they must get the approval from the Student Council for all activity which affected the whole student body."

After four hours of deliberation, Chief Justice Ellis announced to the audience, "We settled as to facts, but we unable to decide as to the law."

A month later the results of the trial were announced. By a 4 to 1 vote, the Student Court upheld the reprimand of the cheerleaders. Before the announced decision, Chief Justice Ellis stated: "We realized the importance of both legislative acts and individual rights, but when the legislature had not infringed upon the judiciary, then there is no reason to declare the act invalid."

Spelling's counsel made a motion for rehearing, which was scheduled after SMU's final exams the following year. However, the rehearing never occurred, as the entire matter was forgotten. Patterson's only statement after hearing the initial verdict was "the decision of the court is most just."

## Life after SMU

Patterson graduated and had a successful law career and was the Senior Partner for approximately 35 years. He was married to his wife Ann, who was a North Dallas High School and SMU graduate, for 47 years. They had two children, Joe Jr. and Amy. Patterson remained active in sports his entire life. He started playing racquetball in his early thirties, but then seeing the folly of his ways, switched to playing handball. After breaking a couple of fingers playing handball (Handball rule No. 1 – the wall always wins), his finger was set improperly by a physician and was in the shape of the letter "L," not like the letter "I" as it should have been. This finger injury ended Patterson's handball playing career.

Patterson then took up distance running, with the Fort Worth Cowtown Marathon as his first lengthy road race. This first race was almost his last race. After a limited training program of short-distance running, Patterson was in no shape to run 26 miles in near-freezing temperatures with mixed rain and sleet. He was treated at the medical tent after finishing about two-thirds of the race. In the years that followed, Patterson finished about six marathons. When full marathons became more of a physical challenge, Patterson assembled four-person marathon teams that competed in the Dallas White Rock Marathon. As his age advanced, Patterson moved to triathlon competition, where he had some limited success in his age bracket. However, he was never the highest ranked individual in his age bracket because one individual, who was a year older, beat him by at least five minutes in every event.

## Restoring the School Spirit Mechanism

Patterson's biggest passion during the last ten years of his life was his quest to restore SMU's school spirit mechanism. After leading SMU to its highest level of overall school spirit, Patterson was appalled by the lack of what he perceived to be the level of the current student loyalty to and spirit at SMU.

In 2009, Redwine started meeting with SMU students and administrators in a mission reminiscent of the mission of Don Quixote. All I could do was admire his effort and his love of SMU. He first met with then Athletic Director Steve Orsini, who played football at Notre Dame, knew a lot about school spirit and the importance of sports tradition at an American university. Orsini was also starting his own mission to infuse more spirit into the SMU student body. Orsini was quick to pick up on Patterson's school spirit and his motive. After about an hour, with Orsini writing down what it seemed to be hundreds of ideas on multiple pages of a flip chart, Orsini was ready to meet with Dr. Lori White, then Vice President for Student Affairs. It was a short meeting. In a follow-up meeting with Patterson, Orsini reported that the personable White

*Patterson scratches his back before a handball game about a year before his career-ending hand injury*

had rejected all of Orsini's spirit ideas. White told Orsini that SMU school spirit had to be generated by students and not by outsiders. Not even an SMU Athletic Director could help to improve school spirit at SMU.

Patterson decided to do what Orsini failed to accomplish in his meeting with White: get the student body more involved with school spirit. Patterson and I.T. Hurst had been thrown out of Jim Caswell's, Dr. Lori White's predecessor, office years before when the two ex-cheerleaders were on the same quest. Almost a year after Orsini's meeting, Patterson met with Dr. White and had the same fate as Steve Orsini. Apparently, getting an appointment with White was like trying to get through the cobweb passageway in George Lucas's movie, "Indiana Jones and the Last Crusade." People knew her office held the Holy Grail but going through the passage to get the Holy Grail was no small task. There were a lot of "dead bodies" on the path who didn't get Dr. White's blessing regarding SMU student spirit.

Through additional advice from Jay Miller, Executive Director of Student Publications, Patterson's next approach was to meet with presidents of the SMU student body to urge them to focus on restoring more spirit at SMU football and basketball games. For the next four years, Patterson met with Jake Torres, Austin

Prentice, Alex Mace, and Ramon Trespalacios. With the help and encouragement of Jennifer Jones, Executive Director for Student Life, Patterson spoke at an SMU Student Senate Meeting, and an AARO (Academic Advising, Registration, & Orientation) incoming freshman parent/student meeting.

On April 5, 2011, at the Student Senate meeting, Patterson spoke for about fifteen minutes about the importance of school spirit for SMU students. After his presentation, Redwine received a standing ovation from the assembled senators. One senator who heard the presentation was future student body president Ramon Trespalacios. Two years later Trespalacios would take Patterson's inspirational message to heart and put the school spirit message into action.

Patterson also spoke to a group of incoming freshmen and their parents at an August 2012 AARO meeting. AARO meetings are scheduled during summer sessions to inform freshman and their parents about student life at SMU. Topics range from rape prevention to the dangers of drug and alcohol abuse. Patterson opened his presentation on school spirit by saying the reason the cheerleading portion of the program was led by such an old cheerleader was that he was "the only ex-cheerleader released from prison who could present." The parents of the freshmen students appeared somewhat perplexed by the prison comment but seemed to accept the comment on the large number of SMU cheerleaders being incarcerated in Huntsville. After the program had ended, the SMU staff at the AARO event spoke highly of the Patterson presentation. But some freshman parents still appeared somewhat confused about why an 80-year-old ex-cheerleader was giving a presentation on school spirit. The parents could have been expecting an extroverted, cute, petite, 18-year-old blond to perform a couple of standing backflips and lead them in a rousing rendition of the "Pony Battle Cry."

As mentioned, Patterson's quest for better student spirit came to fruition after Trespalacios was elected SMU's Student Body President for the 2013-2014 school year. In 2013, SMU's Jennifer Jones told Redwine that Trespalacios was the student body president that he had been looking for four long years. Trespalacios was the right man at the right time, and he capitalized on the excitement

*Ramon Trespalacios and Joe Redwine Patterson, 2015*

over Larry Brown's hire as SMU's head basketball coach and the stud basketball players that Brown recruited from across the country. Trespalacios organized the SMU MOB and donned the only all red outfit he had brought with him from Mexico – the "Lobster Mobster" costume. The lobsterman was seen leading the cheers at all the SMU home basketball games. Moody Magic had returned. Unfortunately, the magic has yet to return to the Gerald Ford football stadium.

Christina Cox, editor-in-chief of the *SMU Campus* Weekly interviewed Patterson in his Dallas home for an article in the February 4, 2016, issue of the paper titled "Alumnus' Spirit Stands Strong." The opening paragraph of her article reads:

> Among a pile of memorabilia, newspaper cuttings, and photos sits a man some would call SMU's biggest fan of the past century. He is one of SMU Athletics' biggest supporters and has lobbied for more school spirit for the past 20 years. Joe Redwine Patterson's love of SMU runs as deep in his veins as it does through his home.

One of the last times I saw Patterson, he was in an Alzheimer's unit of the Belmont Village in Dallas, Texas. It was Father's Day 2016. He was behind a secure door down a long hallway in a large room with five or six other residents who were waiting for their

*From behind the SMU student section, the author and Patterson check on SMU school spirit by sitting behind the SMU student section at a 2015 SMU football game*

lunch. Joe was slumped over in a wheelchair about five feet from a clean table of prepared food. He was wearing tan shorts with a nice clean blue shirt. Both his legs are bandaged with a white gaze on his calves, but it was not possible to see the extent of the injuries. Joe Junior, his son, later said that the injuries were minor cuts caused by getting in and out of bed. On his head was a red SMU baseball cap pulled down so you had to bend down just to see his face. "Joe," I said," Happy Father's Day." I bent down to hear his reply, which was a rambling sentence or two that was unrelated to my question. "Is there anything that I can bring you?" was my next question. In a barely audible reply, I heard," Can you get me a beer?" I replied that I would try to smuggle in a beer or two the next time I came to visit. After a couple of minutes of awkward conversation, he asked, "Is there a game today?" "No Joe," I said. "The first game is not until September when SMU opens with North Texas in Denton." "Let me know when they play so I can watch" were his last understandable words. Then I turned and slowly walked out of the room.

Five: Joe Redwine Patterson

Approximately six months later, on January 6, 2017, Joe Redwine Patterson died at the age of 89 years. Forty years earlier between handball games on a downtown Dallas YMCA handball court, Redwine had told me what he wanted on his tombstone: "Joe Red is Dead." I haven't driven to DeLeon, Texas, to see if his wish is carved in stone.

# Chapter Six
# 1947 Mustang Players

## SMU Favored in Coast Tilt

*"The Mustangs' first intersectional game of the season will be broadcast today at 4:20 over KRLD by Humble Oil Co. Favored by the sports writers all over the country, the Mustangs were given a rousing send-off by the male cheerleader quintet and faithful followers at Union Terminal, Wednesday afternoon, before embarking for the Golden Gate City and Kezar Stadium. The Mustangs are favored because of the return of tailback Doak Walker and the eligibility of Gilbert Johnson, another tailback, who is noted for his passing ability. Other first and second string candidates have added to the strength of the improved Pony squad now that they are in their sophomore year on the Hilltop. Many observers believe teams are in for a rude awakening when the Mustangs take the field in a romping and stomping mood, reminiscent of better years. The team will be welcomed back Tuesday morning at 7:50 by a pep rally at the terminal, Joe Patterson announced Friday."*

The preceding captioned picture of the SMU 1947 Football team was a request of 1947 player Frank Payne. Payne wanted all the players of the 1947 SMU team mentioned in this book. In reviewing the names of players in the photograph, there are some discrepancies such as unnamed players, and duplicate names of players associated with the team photo. After seventy-years, it was impossible to track down corrections to match names with pictures. The full 1947 SMU squad roster is listed in Appendix A as it was printed in the 1948 Cotton Bowl program.

The profile of the SMU 1947 football squad is quite different from the profile of today's college football teams. The biggest difference was the fact that most of the 1947 SMU team served in the military in World War II. In today's college football programs, very few players have any military experience in their backgrounds. Most of the 1947 SMU squad had either had been in the Marines or the Navy. World War II service time also applied to many SMU

First Row: Page, Reinking, Cook, Halliday, Ramsey, McKissack, Stell, Rosenblum
Second Row: Roberts, Lewis, Hill, Roberts, Weatherford, Blackburn, Blakeley, Goodwin, Sutphin
Third Row: Duke, Fikes, Wales, Milam, Pechal, Johnson, Moon, Payne, Basham
Fourth Row: Morton, Adams, Halliday, King, Wallace, Blackburn, Cheney, Adair
Fifth Row: Johnson, Burress, Mizell, Parker, Parker, Sullivan, Cook, Grantham, Moseley
Sixth Row: Moxley, Clark, Marion, Lipke, Russell, Kendrick, Adair, Davis, Richardson
Seventh Row: Cranfill, Perry, Gravis, Gray, Owen, Rosenblum, Martin, Green, Folsom
Eight Row: Hamburger, Walker, Ethridge

cheerleaders and football coaches. Because of their time spent in the military, most SMU football players were in their early- to mid-twenties when they played football for the Mustangs in 1947. Many of the 1947 players were married, and a pro football team already had drafted one player. Several of the team's players came to SMU straight out of high school. This diversity of backgrounds among the football squad was an additional challenge for the SMU coaches and the university.

In profiling players on the SMU 1947 squad, I had the difficult task of selecting which players to highlight in *Glory on the Hilltop*.

After reviewing the 1948 *Rotunda*, I selected those SMU players who had a player picture in the *Rotunda*. Certainly, football lettermen contribute more to a team because of their time on the field than a third-string player. But the contribution to a football team also can be more than playing time in a game. Even a walk-on player can contribute to a team's success.

It has been seventy years since the 1947 SMU football season and only two players, Frank Payne and John Hamberger, could be located to be interviewed for this book.

# Bob Ramsey, Blocking Back, Tri-Captain, Senior

*Senior Tri-Captain Bob Ramsey*

A Dallas resident, Bob Ramsey grew up in East Dallas and played football at Woodrow Wilson High School. He was named to the All-City team in 1940 and 1941. He graduated high school in 1942 and played on the SMU freshman team that year. Recruited into the Navy, Bob spent the next three years as a Navy pilot in the Pacific. He returned to SMU in 1946 to play blocking back, but broke his arm and needed a metal plate inserted. According to the *SMU Campus* newspaper, his favorite leisure activities were swimming, fishing, frogging, and women. An eclectic list to be sure although the SMU newspaper did not list Ramsey's leisure activities in order of preference. The *SMU Campus* noted that Ramsey sometime went by the moniker of the "albino type roadrunner." His most noted quote in the *SMU Campus* was "I like food, especially cooked."

Ramsey graduated in 1948 and majored in banking and finance. He was a member of the "M' Association and Lambda Chi Alpha fraternity.

# Earl Cook, Right Guard, Tri-Captain, Senior

*Earl Cook pictured in 1948 Rotunda*

Earl Cook graduated from Sunset High School in Dallas in 1943. While at Sunset. he lettered in football for three years and in basketball for two years. In his senior year at Sunset High, Cook was named All-City, All-State, and All-Southern in football. After high school, he went into the Marines but was discharged because of a bad knee. The *SMU Campus* reported that Cook had a "strange fascination for tiny petite blondes." By today's point of view, however, there doesn't seem to be any strangeness to this fascination at all. Cook's highlighted the quote in the *SMU Campus* was "I never do anything funny." His most noted story reported by the *SMU Campus* was that he coached the Kappa football team in the spring of 1946 against the Pi Phis. If the SMU Kappa's of 1946 were anything like the SMU Kappa's of the 1960's, Cook was in the right place to help fulfill at least some of his not-so-strange fascinations.

Cook graduated in 1948 with a degree in physical education. He was also a member of "Cycen Fjodr," a special group composed of the ten most outstanding men in the senior class. These men were known as knights, and each knight could select a first-year student to be his serf throughout the year. Duties of the serfs were somewhat vague, and "Cycen Fjodr" is no longer an organization at SMU. Cook also was in SMU's Who's Who listing, a *Rotunda* favorite, and a member of the "M" Association.

# Sid Halliday, Right End, Tri-Captain, Senior

*Sid Halliday heads downfield*

Sid Halliday seemed to have more football playing experience with different football teams than the legendary Fred Ekmark of Texas A&I fame.

Ekmark's most famous quote was that he once told the head coach of a team he was playing for, "I'll only play for your school if I only play games and don't practice." The coach agreed.

After two years of playing high school football at Dallas Woodrow Wilson, Sid played junior college football at Schreiner Junior College even though he appeared on the roster as a high school senior. Halliday left SMU as a freshman so he could get a job and buy a ring for his wife of three years, Joan Malloy. As a four-year veteran of the Marines, Sid also played football with the Marine All-Stars in Hawaii.

Halliday graduated in 1948 and majored in business. He was a *Rotunda* favorite, a member of the "M" Association, and was named All-Southwest Conference for the 1947 football season.

In 2004, Halliday was inducted into the Texas High School Football Hall of Fame. It took approximately sixty-years but his achievements at Woodrow Wilson high school were recognized. His greatest award, however, came from his coach Matty Bell who said, "Sid was what they called today a tight end. That was because he was a fine blocker and a good receiver too. He was the ideal captain, a great leader. We had war veterans and a 17-year-old freshman on that squad, and Sid kept them in a good frame of mind every week. He had consistency."

# Dick McKissack, Fullback, Sophomore

Dick McKissack was part of the magical SMU backfield of 1947

Dick McKissack played football at Thomas Jefferson High School in San Antonio, where he lettered in football and basketball multiple years. Upon graduation in 1944, McKissack joined the Navy. After playing football for a Navy team in San Diego, McKissack spent time in the Carolinas, the Gilberts, and at Okinawa. Listed among his favorite activities were basketball, swimming, dancing, and liking to ride a spirited horse. As a business major, McKissack graduated from SMU in 1950.

# John Hamberger, Right Tackle, Junior

*Hamberger was a stalwart of the 1947 SMU line*

Another product of Dallas Sunset High School, John Hamberger graduated in 1942. In 1941, Hamberger was named All-City and All-State in football. Hamberger then went to the University of Texas, Austin, where he played on the freshman football team. Drafted into the Navy, he spent the next three years as a radio operator in the Pacific. Hamberger came to SMU upon leaving the Navy. His most noted quote in the *SMU Campus* was "Things are always pretty dull. The most exciting thing that ever happened to me was getting out of the Navy."

While at SMU, Hamberger was a member of Lambda Chi Alpha fraternity. He also was First Team All-Southwest Conference in 1947.

*Playing both sides of the line, Hamberger excelled in his career as a tackle at SMU*

After graduating from SMU, Hamberger went on to coach football at Schreiner College in Kerrville, Texas, with ex-SMU coach Rusty Russell. Back in the 1950's, there was a strong football connection between Schreiner Junior College and SMU. An example was Raymond Berry who played at Schreiner before transferring to SMU. Berry went on to have his jersey number retired at SMU and is in the NFL Hall of Fame. Hamberger also coached high school football in Grand Prairie, Texas, and Irving, Texas, and finished his teaching as an administrator in the Irving school district.

Hamberger still stays in touch with former SMU football players, including All-American guard John LaGrone and defensive back Pat Gibson, who both played for the Ponies in the 1967 Cotton Bowl. Hamberger also spoke of how well the SMU players were treated when he played for the Ponies seventy years ago. With a twinkle in his eye, Hamberger asked if I could answer the following trivia question.

> What college football player blocked for both Doak Walker and Tom Landry? The answer, of course, is John Hamberger. John said, "I was just fortunate. Played with Doak. Played with Tommy. What more can you ask?"

At the publishing of this book, John resides in Irving, with his wife Sarah of 63 years. Also in the household is their dog of ten years — the always barking, Matty Bell.

# Floyd "Brownie "Lewis, Left Guard, Junior

*The hard-charging Brownie Lewis*

Known by his nickname "Brownie," Lewis graduated in 1942 from the Masonic Home in Ft. Worth, where he played football and lettered in track. His honors in football included being named All-District and All-State in 1941. Although he started at SMU in 1942, he joined the Marines and served for three years. In the Marines, Brownie made three landings – Bougainville, New Guinea, Iwo Jima, and Guam. Somewhat in the spirit of Winston Groom's character Forrest Gump, Lewis stated that when he retired from his life's work he wanted to own a shrimp boat. Did Winston Groom think there were a lot of individuals that grew up in the South, played college football, served in the military, and had a strange fascination of shrimping?

## Joe Ethridge, Left Tackle, Junior

*Joe Ethridge as pictured in the 1948 Rotunda*

After graduating from Kermit High School in 1945, Ethridge lettered two years in football, two years in basketball, and one year in track. Affectionately known as "the hermit from Kermit," Ethridge often talked about his hometown and even claimed that "after you've seen Japan and the Kermit carnival, you've seen everything." The tradition of bragging about your small Texas hometown seems to be in the DNA of many SMU students. Even in the

1960s, SMU Student Roy Hohl would talk about his hometown of Tomball, Texas. Throughout his time at SMU, Roy was simply known as "Tomball" by his college fraternity brothers. Another odd mystery of the 1940s was the applied term "road-runner." Ethridge was not a "road-runner," but other members of the 1947 team were "road-runners."

# Cecil Sutphin, Center, Senior

Cecil Sutphin of the 1947 Mustangs

Cecil graduated from Goose Creek High School in 1942, but because of bad eyesight, he never served in the military. The only thing that allowed him to play football at SMU was his ability to wear contact lenses. A personal misconception was thinking contact lens only came in vogue in the United States in the 1960s. However, in 1887, Louis J. Girard invented a scleral form of contact lens.

By all written accounts, Sutphin was somewhat of a "renaissance man" who perfected a lot of different talents at a young age. At one time, *The Dallas Morning News* labeled Sutphin as the "usual

*Cecil Sutphin being carried off the Cotton Bowl field with a broken leg*

buffoon." Sutphin was known by the nickname "Crooner" as he wrote the song, "Oleander Trail" at the age of fourteen. He sang "Oleander Trail" with local bands until he graduated from high school. Cecil then went on a singing tour across the south, but shortly tired of the tour life and sang in a nightclub in California for the next two years.

Sutphin developed a love of football at an early age. At the age of five, Cecil broke his collarbone playing sandlot football with kids twice his age. Against his mother's wishes, he played high school football at Goose Creek, where in his senior year he was co-captain of the football team and named All-District. Coming to SMU in 1944, Cecil had lettered in football for the past three seasons. The most remarkable fact about Sutphin's football career at SMU was that he weighed only 165 pounds on a six-foot-two frame. Although he played center, having someone of his stature in this position is a lost concept in today's college football game. Most football coaches don't want a quick and tall player playing center, but rather prefer slow, heavy players who usually cover a short distance from where they center the ball.

The other aspect of center play is usually the center's play is not noticed unless the center miss snaps the long snap. In the single-wing formation, every snap is usually into the backfield. Sutphin, in the 1947 SMU/TCU game, had two bad snaps. In the opinion of some SMU fans, the two bad snaps contributed greatly to the game's 19-19 tie.

The most interesting play of Sutphin's SMU career was breaking his leg near the end of play in the 1948 Cotton Bowl. That injury was his last play as an SMU player.

As described in *The Dallas Morning News*, after the game, the SMU players "pushed their way through the throng into their buses for the trip back to the Methodist campus where they changed into street attire." Sutphin was the first

Before boarding the bus, someone helped Cecil lean on a fender of a car parked in the tunnel of the Cotton Bowl. Leaning on the car, he witnessed the final two minutes of play. Sutphin mumbled to a nearby sympathizer, "We still got time to lick them." But as time expired in the game, his only comment was, "Get me back on the bus."

# Dick Reinking, Left End, Senior

Dick Reinking of the 1947 Mustangs

Reinking grew up in the Dallas area and graduated from Lancaster High School in 1944. He lettered two years in football at Lancaster and was All-District in 1943.

The Daily Campus reported that Reinking went by the nickname "Zephryhead," and had John L. Lewis eyebrows with a build like Atlas. It also was reported that he would sing "Ride the Train to Glory" with Bob Ramsey. Reinking was a finance major and graduated in 1948.

Dick Reinking was also a member of the "M" Association, and a member of Kappa Sigma Fraternity.

# Paul Page, Wing Back, Junior

*Paul Page heads downfield*

The junior wing back, Paul Page was from Eldorado, Texas, located 43 miles south of San Angelo. Eldorado has always been a small town, with the 2009 population of about 1,800. Page was the youngest of six children. He was a natural athlete in high school and lettered three years in football, basketball, and track, and played tennis. One year, he participated in a district track and tennis meet, with all events on the same day. Paul also excelled in academics and was the salutatorian of his senior class.

Page's older brother Wilson attended SMU, so he set his mind on attending SMU and playing football. When assistant coach Rusty Russell came to El Dorado to recruit Page, Russell already had a scholarship offer for Page in his pocket. Page had told Russell two things before making the scholarship offer: He was going to SMU, and he wanted to play football. The scholarship offer never left Russell's pocket, and Page attended SMU and played freshman football as a "walk-on" his freshman year. Paul was given a football scholarship for his sophomore through senior years.

Page had a brilliant football career at SMU. He led the team in rushing in 1945 and 1946. Not only was Page an offensive player, but he also was a great defensive back. It took more than forty years to beat his record fifteen interceptions in his SMU career, seven interceptions in a single season, and three interceptions in a single game (vs. Texas A&M 1947). Pages also led the Ponies in interceptions in 1947 and 1948. Page's two key offensive plays in 1947 were his opening kickoff return against the University of Texas and his 86-yard pass reception from Gilbert Johnson against UCLA.

The *SMU Campus* noted that Paul was one of the few players on the 1947 team to wear low-top football shoes. The *SMU Campus* went on to say that low-top shoes were the exciting new trend in football shoes. At SMU, Page was also a Blue Key member and a member of Cycen Fjodr Honorary Society.

## Respect for Doak Walker

Paul Page also had a great respect for teammate Doak Walker. In a 1995 article in the San Angelo Standard-Times, Page said of his teammate, "Doak was the best player I ever saw. Playing with Doak was the highlight of my career. I still talk to him every six months or so…"

## Life after SMU

Page graduated in January 1949 from SMU and married his college sweetheart Lucy Huckaby in February 1949. That spring, Paul went to work for Northwest Lumber Company in Dallas. Ex-SMU'ers Harlan Ray and Fritz Hawn owned the company. In 1949, as a first-round draft pick in both the National Football League and the American Football League, Page joined the Baltimore Colts. He had a successful year as a starter on both offense and defense, but his first pro-football year ended with a broken leg late in the season.

After one year with the Baltimore Colts, Page hung up his low-top football shoes and called it a career. Upon returning to Dallas to work, Page found the ties to West Texas were too strong, and in 1951 he went to West Texas for ranching and later start his oil company, Page Energy. He later served as a Trustee of Schreiner College and served as a Director of the First National Bank of Eldorado for twenty-one years. Among Page's honors is the SMU

Sports Hall of Fame in 1981 and the Distinguished Alumni Award from SMU in 1993.

The essence of Paul Page's character is captured in his favorite quote, "The quality of a man's life is in direct proportion to his striving for excellence."

# Gilbert Johnson, Tailback, Sophomore

*The "Old Man" of the 1947 squad drops back to pass*

What could be more different on a football team in the 1940s than having a back who was known only for his passing and wore jersey number forty-five? From Tyler Texas, Gilbert Johnson played and lettered in football for three years. He then went to summer school at Texas A&M before going into the Navy from 1942 to 1946. In the Navy, Johnson served in the submarine service in the Pacific for twenty-six months. Johnson was twenty-four years old when he started at SMU in 1946. Because of his receding hairline and age, Johnson earned the nickname of "the old man." Johnson got even somewhat with the nicknames as he called Frank Payne "the Younger." When Johnson arrived at SMU, he was assigned to a room with Francis Pulatti. Johnson first thought that this was his lucky day, but Francis turned out to be just another football player on the team. Roommates of the opposite sex did not to come into vogue until the 1990s, and choosing one's gender for the semester did not become popular until around 2015.

In 1949, Johnson played one year of professional football with the New York Yankees. For many years, he ran an Exxon station in Dallas. Johnson died in 1999 at the age of 75.

# Frank Payne, Wing Back, Sophomore

Frank Payne Senior, 1923 SMU Team (left) and Frank Payne, Junior, 1947 SMU Team (right)

Frank Payne was a West Texas native who came to SMU graduating from Breckenridge High School, about 30 miles west of Fort Worth. Payne was a wingback and tailback at Breckenridge High School. Unfortunately, Payne broke his leg his senior year and, therefore, was not heavily recruited by most colleges. Payne's father, Frank Payne Sr., played at SMU from 1921 to 1923 and lettered in football. Payne has the distinction of being the first second-generation SMU player to letter in football. Not only were the Payne's the first father-son football letterman for the Mustangs, they also were the only father-son players to play on undefeated SMU teams.

Frank senior was on the undefeated Ray Morrison team (9-0-0) in 1923, and son Frank was on the undefeated Mustang team (9-0-2) in 1947.

During his junior and senior years at SMU, Payne received a lot more playing time than he did in the 1947 season. He also emerged as one of the football teams' leaders for the 1948 and 1949 squads. Payne also coached the 1952 SMU freshman team with Coach Tom

*Frank Payne Jr., another great talent in the backfield of the 1947 Mustangs*

Dean. Like all running backs in the Doak Walker years, Payne had a strong relationship with Doak Walker. He was seen pictured with Walker at the occasion of the first Doak Walker Award presented in 1990.

After graduation from SMU in 1950, Frank attended Southwestern Medical School in Dallas and later become a noted pediatrician in the Dallas area. Payne practiced medicine in Dallas until 2004, when he retired from his medical career.

*Frank Payne and Doak Walker*

A visit to Payne's North Dallas home near SMU is a showcase of facts and memorabilia of SMU 1940s and 1950s football. Payne still attends SMU football games and can be spotted on the Boulevard before most games. With his wife, Jane, and multiple cats; Payne is still not taking it easy. Payne works out regularly and his biceps are larger than most men that are twenty years younger.

Payne is a great example of the character and the work ethic of the players on the 1947 SMU football team.

# Chapter Seven
# SMU Spirit and Cheerleaders

*Patterson, Hurst, Herkimer, Pappadas, Tartt*

SMU School Spirit peaked in the Doak Walker era. Many of the spirit events and organizations disappeared from SMU by the late 1950s. In 1947, the spirit of SMU and Texas A&M University were very much the same at both schools. Both schools had bonfires, pep rallies before the games, an engaged student body that supported the school, and alumni who were proud of their school. Alumni attended and supported school athletics years after they graduated from their respective schools. The Aggies continue many of their spirit traditions even today, but SMU relegated most of its spirit traditions as outdated or no longer important to the SMU student experience on the Hilltop.

When Patterson was campaigning to restore SMU's "school spirit mechanism," many SMU administrators told him that "SMU

The forgotten SMU spirit group the "Blue Shirts."

SMU pre-game bonfire
Pictured is the symbolic roasting of a Razorback

*Peruna looks tired and one SMU cheerleader is walking backward in downtown Dallas in the 1947 SMU Homecoming Parade*

students have more to learn at the University than spending time with out-of-date SMU school traditions of the past." Dr. Lori White, Vice President of Student Affairs, also stated, "We are SMU and not Texas A&M."

## The SMU Blue Shirts

The Blue Shirts were a men's spirit organization for freshmen in the 1940s, but by the late 1950s, the Shirts were no more. Their numbers ranked as high as 120 during the Doak Walker glory days. The Blue Shirts participated in pep rallies and sat as a group at SMU home football games. Many Blue Shirts even attended away football games to cheer for the Ponies.

*An SMU pep rally in 1947*

*Patterson challenges the 1947 SMU faithful*

Filling the Stadium was never a problem in the 1947 season

## The 1947 SMU Cheerleaders

There were five male cheerleaders on the 1947 SMU cheerleading squad. Joe Redwine Patterson was elected head cheerleader by popular vote by the SMU student body. Patterson appointed the four remaining cheerleaders. Of those four cheerleaders, only Lawrence Herkimer was a returning cheerleader. Herkimer was head cheerleader of the SMU squad in 1946 and also was a head cheerleader in 1943. The other 1946 cheerleaders were Al Hughes, Gloria Feitler, Mary Lou Sanford, and Wesley Porter. SMU's first female cheerleader was Anna Bell Newman, who was part of the first cheerleading squad in 1915. In 1915, if anyone could be a cheerleader at SMU. No elections and appointments were necessary. An article in the *SMU Campus* described the 1947 squad.

"Mustangs Fight! This familiar and rousing cheer heard each year from the stands at Mustang football games will be prompted this season by five hustling cheerleaders. Joe

*How high can these 1947 cheerleaders jump? They're all off the ground*

Patterson of Graham, elected by popular student vote to be a head cheerleader at SMU, will head a group of five male yell rousers. The other four members of the group, who were appointed by Patterson, are I. T. Hurst, Dallas; Blake Tartt, Houston; Tasos Pappadas, Houston, and Lawrence Herkimer, Dallas. Herkimer is serving his second season with the popular group. Last year Herkimer served as a head cheerleader. Uniforms and equipment for the group was furnished free through the graciousness of several Dallas merchants. The merchants making contributions to the group are Jas. K. Wilson, Titche-Goettinger, Volk, Reynolds-Penland, and Dreyfuss & Son. The group, always a popular aggregation on the campus, may be found this season at various times of the day or night supervising pep rallies and bonfires. Special pep rallies will be on the bill-of-fare preceding each football game. The male quintet requests that all students be present at the rallies. The next rally will be held at 7:50 a.m. Tuesday, at the Union Terminal. The event will hail the return of the Mustang football squad from California. The group will lead the Mustang rooting section at all future Pony games with possibly the exception

*The only known photo of SMU cheerleaders balancing on a goalpost*

of the U.C.L.A. contest, which will be played on the coast. Patterson said he hopes that all the members will be able to travel to California for this game, but that is still in doubt."

The 1948 cheerleading squad was led by the popular Aaron Spelling, later of Hollywood fame. The rest of the cheerleaders were Marc Moore, Jim Gobel, Hugh Frye, and Johnny Rudin. There was a high degree of competitiveness among the three SMU head cheerleaders of 1946, 1947, and 1948. The large egos of the head cheerleaders contributed to this competitiveness. The SMU head cheerleader was the focal point of the SMU student body because football was the primary SMU school sport at the time. There were no women sports listed in the 1947 *Rotunda*. Women did have intercollegiate sport at SMU from 1915-1924 but in 1924, SMU decided to move all women's athletics to an intramural program. The *SMU Campus* included weekly write-ups on the women's

*1947 Cheerleaders Going Home after a Bonfire*

intermural games. How important was SMU college football in 1947? Ask any 1947 SMU alumni about their memories of SMU spirit and their description is usually one word "Redwine." But more than just Patterson and the other cheerleaders, Alumni from 1947 and 1948 remember the lucky, magical, and spirited SMU football season of 1947.

## A Season of Cheering

For the five SMU cheerleaders of 1947, it was a season of cheering that ended their activity as a cheerleader. The only cheerleader who was involved with cheerleading after the 1947 season was Lawrence Herkimer, who started cheerleading camps and went on to start Cheerleader Supply, a successful company that sold pom poms and cheerleading outfits to little girls who dreamed of cheering on Pee Wee, junior high, and high school football teams. All the 1947 cheerleaders went on to successful careers after their graduation from SMU.

The 1947 cheerleading squad was special primarily because of its association with the 1947 football team. In the remodeled Moody Coliseum, there is a mural of a picture depicting the five

*Patterson poses in front of cheerleader pyramid in Moody Coliseum*

cheerleaders from 1947. Another picture showing the cheerleaders in a pyramid is located with other SMU sports memorabilia in an alcove on the north side near the front of Moody Coliseum. However, one must buy an $8 beer from vendors at a portable beer stand to get a good view of the mural. Additional information on Patterson's four selected cheerleader assistants follows.

## I.T. Hurst, Senior, Dallas, TX

Ira Talmadge (I.T.) Hurst was the perfect candidate to be a cheerleader at SMU in 1947. Born in Dallas in 1924, Hurst graduated from North Dallas High School in 1942. He attended SMU for a semester before going into the Army and serving in the Pacific serving in New Caledonia and the Philippines. Like many World War II veterans, Hurst saw more of the world that he expected to see and unfortunately was exposed to the horrors of war. And like a lot of SMU student veterans, Hurst returned to the place of his roots – Dallas and SMU. According to Patterson, another reason that Hurst returned to SMU that he couldn't wait to get back home to "date all them pretty SMU girls."

After re-enrolling at SMU, Hurst joined the local chapter of ATO fraternity. Although Patterson was not in a fraternity, he knew

I.T. with future wife, Pat Newman

he had to get buy-in from the Greek community to increase SMU spirit. Total student body participation was the only thing that would get SMU school spirit to work. Patterson turned to fraternities to find volunteers for the 1947 cheerleading squad. The ATOs at SMU had a long history of their members being cheerleaders, and two of the volunteers, Blake Tartt and Hurst were roommates in the ATO fraternity house. At that time, the cheerleaders were Peruna's handlers. What could have been better for a few SMU frat men than to lead cheers in front of beautiful SMU co-eds and to handle a miniature horse at the same time?

Although he never played football growing up in Dallas, Hurst had a deep love of football. He carried that love of football,

*I.T. Hurst's S.M.U. License Plate*

SMU, and the ATO fraternity for his entire life. After graduation from SMU, Hurst got his first job at General Motors Acceptance Corporation (GMAC) in Dallas. Although his GMAC job would take him to romantic, faraway places like Argentina, his GMAC job also took him to the unromantic place of Northern Louisiana. Hurst had always wanted to sell cars, so he returned to Dallas and spent the rest of his working career in the automobile business.

Hurst maintained his strong love for SMU throughout his life. He would take his son Robert to every football and basketball game that he could attend. When personalized license plates became available in Texas in 1971, Hurst ordered a plate with "S.M.U." After he died, Robert had the license plate transferred to his name. Hurst and Patterson frequently roamed the stadium at SMU home football games to check on "the school spirit mechanism." Hurst was thrown out of countless SMU school administrator offices for being overzealous for the "Red and the Blue."

In 2002, it was Patterson who convinced Hurst to go to the hospital when he was experiencing chest pains. Unfortunately, he never recovered enough to leave the hospital. Hurst was one of the few SMU alumni to have their funeral service in Perkins Chapel on the SMU campus. As Wilson Pickett would say at "the Midnight

Hour," some of I.T.'s ashes found an eternal resting place in the bushes on the right side of Dallas Hall. With his SMU memorabilia collection, Patterson even had a handwritten sketch of where Hurst's ashes were scattered.

On January 23, 2003, a front-page Daily Campus article titled "Mustangs Lose No. 1 fan." The article proclaimed Hurst as the No. 1 fan of SMU football fan at the time of his death. The first line of the story included a quote from Patterson, "If there was anyone that lived and breathed SMU, then it was I.T." Also in the article, Patterson warmly remembered his friend as a man with an "indomitable soul for SMU school spirit."

## Blake Tartt, Junior, Houston TX

Blake Tartt was born in Houston, Texas, on March 16, 1929. He grew up in Houston and graduated from SMU in 1949. Tartt was a cheerleader only one year, 1947 when he was a junior at SMU. Tartt later went on to the SMU Dedman School of Law and graduated cum laude. He was awarded the Outstanding Senior Law Student Award in 1959. Tartt's time in law school was interrupted when he flew with the 98th Bombardment Wing of the United States Air Force in the Korean War as a First Lieutenant.

To say that Tartt had an extraordinary legal career would be an understatement. After law school, he joined the Houston firm of Fulbright, Crooker, Freeman, Bates, and Jaworski, where he became a senior partner and practiced law for 40 years. Upon his retirement from Fulbright & Jaworski in 2000, he became a partner with Beirne, Maynard & Parsons, where he practiced until his death in 2014. His list of accomplishments and awards in law are too many to be mentioned in this book as the list would span many pages. A short list of Tartt's membership ties included: President of the River Oaks Property Owner's Association, past member of the Board of the Museum of Fine Arts of Houston, a member of the Coronado Club, the Forest Club, the Argyle Club of San Antonio, and the Reform Club of London England.

The following was written about Tartt in his obituary in the *Houston Chronicle*: "In sum, Blake was a true Southern gentleman, widely known for his love of family, his wit and wisdom, a remarkable smile, incredible memory, great intelligence, deep-rooted

*Blake Tartt*

integrity, true friendship, thoughtfulness, and kindness — a man for all seasons." Tartt's epitaph describes very few men living in America today.

## Tasos Pappadas, Senior, Houston TX

Like Tartt, Tasos Pappadas was from Houston, but he was a member of the PKA fraternity at SMU. Tasos went by the nickname of "Pappy," and like the other four cheerleaders expressed a lifelong love for the "ponies from high on the Hilltop." In a 2017 interview, Tasos said that he always wanted to be a cheerleader, but only got the chance his senior year on the Hilltop. Tasos also mentioned the beautiful SMU co-eds, but his father warned him to stay away from those "cute Texas girls" and marry a good Greek girl.

After graduating from SMU in 1948, Pappy returned to Houston to begin a successful career in insurance. Tasos love for SMU didn't end when he graduated. Pappadas was active in helping

*Pappadas as a young successful Houston businessman*

recruit Houston area high school prospects to SMU. Through his involvement with recruitment, he became a friend of then SMU head football coach Hayden Fry. Fry and one of his assistants, Charles Driver, visited Tasos in his home in Houston on many occasions to discuss ways to convince high school students to play football at SMU. Tasos noted that Fry had one of the first Ford Mustangs off the assembly line. The car's colors were, of course, red and blue.

Pappadas also mentioned the difficulties recruiting against the University of Texas and then head football coach Darrell Royal. Tasos stated, "Every star high school football player in Texas wanted to play for Darrell Royal when he coached at "The University." Also, at the time, there was almost an unlimited number of players who could play for a college or university, and the Orange Bloods would recruit as many good players as they could to keep players from going to other Southwest Conference schools. Gary Shaw's classic book of football at U.T. Austin titled, "Meat on the Hoof" describes the practice of "stacking players" who will contribute very little to no game time.

Tasos Pappadas still resides in Houston with his Greek wife, Eunice, of sixty-one years. At the age of 91, Tasos still talks a lot about Pony football. He reflects on seventy years of following the boys on the Hilltop and wonders if Chad Morris can return the Mustangs to their days of glory inspired by Doak Walker, and the great Mustang team of 1947.

## Lawrence Herkimer, Senior, Dallas, TX

Lawrence Herkimer was the only SMU cheerleader of 1947 who did anything with his SMU cheerleading experience as a career. In a New York Times article on March 15, 2009, the Times anointed Herkimer as the "Grandfather of Modern Cheerleading." Herkimer's name was even part of a question on a quiz show: "What profession is most likely to perform a herkie?" In the 1940s, Herkimer created the move at SMU. Patterson always claimed that the move was just to compensate for the lack of Herkimer's jumping ability. But later, however, Herkimer admitted that "it (the Herkie) was just a poor split jump." There was always a friendly rivalry between Patterson and Herkimer. Many SMU graduates in the 1947 and 1948 classes recalled that Patterson failed to attend Herkimer's Dallas funeral, even though Patterson was living in Dallas when Herkimer died and could have easily attended.

Herkimer's wife, the former Dorothy Brown, persuaded Herkimer to start making and selling cheerleader supplies and skirts that she had designed. Herkimer borrowed $600 from a friend of his father-in-law to start his business. In 1948, he started his first cheerleading camp at Sam Houston State Teachers College with 52 girls and one boy. Enrollment soon climbed to 350 per summer camp. Soon, Herkimer was making more money from his summer cheerleading camps and he quit teaching physical education and

*Herkimer is doing the "Herkie"*

statistics at SMU to go into cheerleading full time. He started the National Cheerleaders Association, which became a big business, running camps at 630 sites staffed by 1,500 instructors, and training 150,000 would-be cheerleaders on a yearly basis. SMU would fill most of their college dorms with high school cheerleaders during many of the SMU summer based camps. Herkimer's associate company, Cheerleader Supply Company, however, was the most profitable just by selling sweaters, skirts, pom poms, and specialized uniforms. When Herkimer sold out his companies in 1986, he cashed in for approximately $20 million.

Years later Herkimer worried that cheerleading was too focused on all-star squads and not on cheering for the fans in the stands. Cheerleading also has turned into a sport that is increasingly dangerous. In fact, according to the NCAA, cheerleading is the most injury prone sport in college today.

In the March 15, 2009, edition of *The New York Times*, Herkimer expressed his concerns over the direction in which he thought

*Lawrence Herkimer, SMU's All-Time Best-Known Cheerleader*

cheerleading as a sport was going. Herkimer said, "I'm amazed cheerleading came so far, so I don't know where it could go from here. All I can see is it going downhill. If they stop being an asset to the school and school activities, then cheerleading can die."

Herkimer died on July 1, 2015, of heart failure in Dallas at the age of 89. Services were at Highland Park United Methodist Church in Dallas. Herkimer had served on many local school boards, including the Dallas Independent School Board in the 1960s and on the Hockaday School Board of Trustees.

# Chapter Eight
# Mustang Assistant Coaching Staff

"SMU's 1947 football hopes will be aided by the addition of three new assistant coaches. Herman Cowley, former coach of strong football teams at Dallas' Sunset high school, joined the staff last spring. His elevens won numerous championships and bi-district championships. Clinton McClain, a Mustang star in 1930 and 1940, joined his alma mater in the spring as an assistant coach. He formerly played professional football with the New York Giants and with Jersey City. E. O. (Doc) Hayes will be remembered by most Dallasites as very successful basketball coach from Technical high school. Hayes succeeded Forrest C. Baccus as head basketball coach in the spring. Hayes has been one of the leading grid officials in the Southwest Conference for many years. The record of Madison Bell, director of athletics and head football coach speaks for itself. Bell, starting his tenth season as a head mentor for the Mustangs, will be remembered by his first year as a coach here at the Hilltop. His 1935 team went to the Rose Bowl to be barely defeated by Stanford, 7-0. H. N. (Rusty) Russell, the former Howard Payne great and coach at both the Masonic Home and Highland Park high schools, will play an important part in the athletic set-up. Russell's 1944 Highland Park high school team went to the state finals to be defeated by Port Arthur. McAdoo Keaton, the assistant coach, developed numerous championship elevens at Howard Payne, his alma mater. Keaton is recognized as one of the best line coaches in the conference. With this coaching staff and the material present on the Hilltop. SMU looms as a great threat to defending co-champions from last year, Rice and Arkansas."

## 1947 SMU Football Coaching Staff

The 1947 season started with three new assistant football coaches. The most significant addition to the staff was H.N. (Rusty) Russell who had coached at Highland Park. Matty Bell brought in Russell to create the single-wing offense for the Mustangs. The other significant addition was McAdoo Keaton who was a noted

Bell, Hayes, Russell, Keaton, Cowley, McClain

line coach. In a 2016 interview with 1947 linemen, John Hamberger commented that although other football coaches are in group pictures of SMU coaches' only three — Matty Bell, Rusty Russell, and McAdoo Keaton — coached football daily for the 1947 SMU varsity football team.

## Harvey N. (Rusty) Russell

Rusty Russell's sports career began in Wichita Falls, Texas, playing high school football. Russell went on to play college football at Howard Payne University in Brownwood, Texas. Russell's playing career at Howard Payne was spread over a longer period because he served in the U.S. Army in Europe from 1918-1919 after World War I. He played football for Howard Payne in 1917 and 1920-1921. Russell also played basketball in 1916-1917 and 1921-1922. He graduated with a BA in Education from Howard Payne in 1922. However, Russell's induction into the Howard Payne Sports Hall of Fame did not occur until 1989.

Russell came to SMU with a successful record coaching high school football in Texas. His biggest success was coaching at the

Rusty Russell pictured in the 1948 Rotunda

Masonic Home outside of Ft. Worth. Over a twelve-year stretch, Russell had 111 wins and only twenty-six losses at the Masonic Home. The full story of the Mighty Mites of Masonic Home is in Jim Dent's highly entertaining book, "Twelve Mighty Orphans."

In an article in *Dave Campbell's Texas Football*, former Masonic Home player and a member of the Texas High School Football Hall of Fame, Allie White said of Russell, "Mr. Russell was a master. I think in about ten years the pros will be doing the stuff we did at Masonic Home. He had a way of leading people." Most years, the football team at the Masonic Home only had about twenty-three active players. Rusty Russell had his Mighty Mites memorize between 75 and 100 plays. The Masonic plays included traps, reverses, throwing the ball to everyone who was an eligible receiver, shovel passes, option plays, and sending men in motion. Sometimes even the Mighty Mites on the field didn't know where the ball was going and who was running or passing.

When the Highland Park high school football coach left to go into the service in 1942, Russell left the Masonic Home to go to Highland Park for a lot more money. After Russell had left the Masonic Home, the football program at the Home was never the same. In 1950, Rusty Russell became the head football coach at SMU after Matty Bell became the SMU Athletic Director. Russell coached at SMU for three years and had a 13-15-2 record.

Russell later became head coach at Schreiner Institute and coached at Victoria College. An interesting side note is that John Hamberger, the 1947 SMU tackle, was an assistant coach at Schreiner Institute when Rusty Russell was the head coach at Schreiner Institute.

Rusty Russell was inducted into the Texas High School Football Hall of Fame in 1986 for his coaching at the Masonic Home and Highland Park High School. In 2013, Russell was inducted into the Southwest Conference Hall of Fame. He died in 1983.

## James McAdoo Keaton

Like Russell, McAdoo Keaton also had a deep connection to football at Howard Payne University. Keaton lettered in football in 1918 and 1920-1923. He was an assistant Howard Payne football coach in 1924. Also, Keeton served as an assistant coach at Howard Payne from 1927 to 1934.

Keaton moved up to become the Yellow Jackets' head football coach at in 1935. He was the head coach at Howard Payne from 1935 to 1943. Keaton had an outstanding career as head coach at Howard Payne with a 53-19-8 record. His record at the school placed him second on the all-time list of Yellow Jacket coaches with a winning percentage of .663. In 1964, McAdoo Keaton was the Howard Payne College Man-of-the-Year.

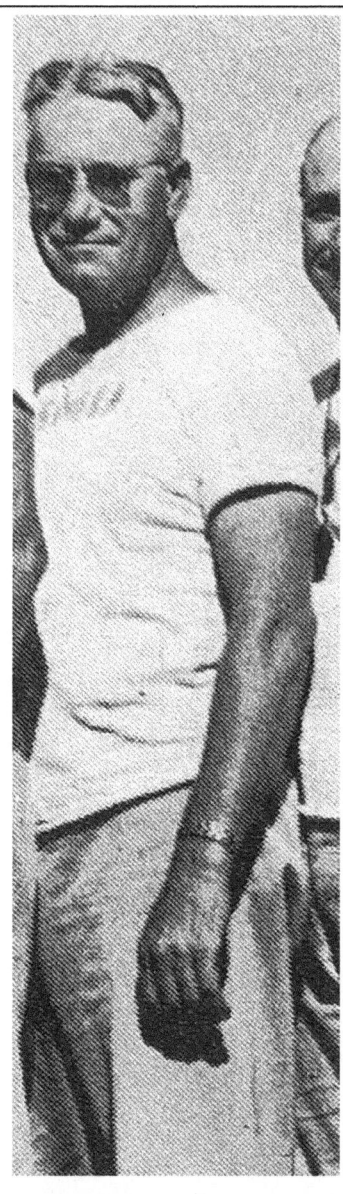

McAdoo Keaton pictured in the 1948 Rotunda

McAdoo Keaton was equally as stellar as SMU's line coach. Keaton also coached track at SMU and took two U.S. national track teams to compete internationally.

# Chapter Nine
# 1947 SMU Season

*"After the first fall practice, the team gathered on the practice field and set a goal of the 1947 season. The Mustang's team goal for the 1947 season was to have an undefeated season and go to the Cotton Bowl."*
— Dr. Frank Payne, 2016

Backfield of Walker, Johnson, Page, and McKissack

*"We were a team of average talent, except for some talented backfield players like Page, Johnson, Payne, and McKissack. Of course, the team had one player by the name of Doak."*
— John Hamberger, 2016

The factors that go into a successful college football season are many: new players' versus returning players, team chemistry, player injuries during the season, loss of players during the season, changes in the coaching staff from one season to the next, and even weather conditions during individual games. To make things even more complicated, your opponents for any season are also undergoing changes from the previous season. A team can beat an opponent 40-0 one year and lose 24-21 the following year.

One of the biggest factors about football, sports, or even in life itself is the element of luck. The football hits the goal post crossbar and either falls forward to victory or falls backward to defeat. A player running down the sideline either steps out of bounds or stays in bounds to score a touchdown, often by what could be a matter of inches. A bad call by a referee changes the outcome of the play or a game.

> Sometimes the element of luck is the deciding factor in determining a national championship. In the Austin College/Concordia NAIA Division II championship game in 1981, the Kangaroos kicked a 57-yard field goal with a 1:12 left on the clock to tie Concordia 24-24 to be the 1981 co-champions. All the Presbyterian Kangaroos in the stands on that cool, cloudy December day in Sherman Texas attributed the kick as being a pre-destined act of God. From the stands, the kick appeared to be at least a foot short. Like nudged by the hand of God the football, however, bounced over the crossbar.

Another element of winning is Geoff Colvin's theory of what separates world-class athletic performers from everyone else. Colvin's theory is that "deliberate practice" makes the difference in performance. Colvin goes into this theory in detail in his book, "Talent is Overrated." Natural talent and hard work may come into consideration for success. However, talent alone is not the major reason for overall success.

The 1946 SMU football team had a 4-5-1 record and finished with a 2-4 record in the Southwest Conference. The Mustangs conference record was only good for a tie for fifth place in the Southwest Conference standings. The Mustangs scored 114 points and had 100 points scored against them in the 1946 season. But, there were some games in the 1946 season that gave some hope that SMU's record would be better the following year. Two big wins occurred at the end of the 1946 season. The Mustangs beat TCU

30-13 and Baylor 35-0, although both games were home games for the Mustangs.

Before the 1947 SMU football season, SMU had only two undefeated seasons. The Ray Morrison teams of 1923 and 1926 went 9-0-0 and 8-0-1.

Although undefeated in the regular season, the 1935 team lost to Stanford in the Rose Bowl. After the 1947 football season, SMU has had only one undefeated team, which was Bobby Collins' team of 1983 that went 11-0-1. The 1947 SMU football team played one of only four seasons of no-loss football on the Hilltop.

The buzz before the 1947 season started was that the Ponies would have a good, but not necessarily great, year. The attitude on campus was best expressed in the *SMU Campus*:

> Let's get that school spirit this year by coming to the football game tonight and cheering our team on to victory," said Joe Patterson, head cheerleader for SMU. Patterson stated that the student body would sit in a mass, in the seats indicated on their tickets, so that the cheering may be organized. "It is our opinion that this school is due a new awakening," continued Patterson, "in that every student should be interested not only in all athletic phases on the campus, but also his studies, student government, and all other activities that relate directly to the school itself." Patterson believes we, as SMU Students, can play a vital part in the outcome of our football team this year by backing them in every possible way. "We have a good football team this year, we have a lot of fine students, and we've got some reasonable facsimiles of yell leaders; therefore, we have all that is necessary to make our team the best in the Southwest Conference, concluded Patterson. Also cheering for the team tonight will be Blake Tartt, I. T. Hurst, "Pappy" Pappadas, and Lawrence Herkimer.

The historical SMU football season began on the road at Kezar Stadium against the Broncos of Santa Clara.

## Game One – Santa Clara Broncos
Attendance 5,000
9/27/1947, Kezar Stadium, San Francisco, CA

*Doak Walker leaves four Broncos' and one referee behind*

The first game of the season came with high expectations for the Mustangs. However, Santa Clara was expected to field a good team in 1947. The Broncos had played a season opener game against California the week before and lost 38-9. Also, they had lost their first-string quarterback, Bill Crowley because of an ankle injury. Santa Clara had a lot of depth, as the Broncos returned twenty-seven lettermen from 1946. The Mustangs had to travel 1,700 miles by train to San Francisco, which was not considered a restful trip even in 1947.

The Broncos had an experienced head coach in Leonard Casanova, who had coached football for 20 years. Casanova claim to fame was that in 1923, as a player, he had punted the distance of 98 yards. In the game called "The Little Big Game," the distance was his one-yard line to the opponent's one-yard line.

The first half of the game was a defensive struggle, with the Ponies only leading 6-0. The Mustangs only score of the half showed the difference Doak Walker could make on the team. Fading back to pass on the Santa Clara 17-yard line, Walker appeared to be trapped by a couple of Broncos, but in Roger Staubach style he dazzled his way to the three-yard line. Fullback Dick McKissack took the ball to the one and on the next play Walker went in for the touchdown.

The second half continued the display of Walker's many football talents. Early in the second half, Walker intercepted a Bronco pass and returned it to the Ponies' 37-yard line. After a good run by McKissack, Walker broke loose for a 44-yard touchdown run. The final SMU score also came from Walker, as he fielded the ball on a kickoff on his four-yard line and, with the help of several great blocks by teammates; he made it to the 50-yard line. From the 50-yard line on, he simply outran the Broncos for a 96-yard touchdown run. Other than this 96-yard touchdown run, Doak Walker's biggest success regarding the Santa Clara game was a date with Jane Russell. Walker's only comment about his date was, "Well she's very nice." The following statistics indicate how close the first game of the season was.

Statistically, for the Mustangs, the Santa Clara game was not a great game. Although the Mustangs intercepted three passes, two of their passes were intercepted. By today's college football standards, eighteen yards passing is almost like not passing at all. It was not

| Statistics, SMU vs. Santa Clara | | |
|---|---|---|
| | SMU | Santa Clara |
| First Downs | 9 | 12 |
| Yards Rushing | 183 | 166 |
| Yards Passing | 18 | 118 |
| Pass Attempts | 12 | 21 |
| Pass Completes | 3 | 19 |
| Passes Intercepted | 3 | 2 |
| Fumbles Recovered | 0 | 0 |
| Punting Average | 43.2 | 28.2 |
| Yards Penalized | 19 | 25 |

until the fourth quarter that the Mustangs broke open the Santa Clara game open. Looking back after almost seventy years, the Santa Clara/SMU game of 1947 appeared to be an easy win for the Ponies. Return yardage on kickoffs and punts was a big factor in the SMU victory. A first game win for the season was a great thing, especially since the Ponies had to travel halfway across the country to obtain it.

**Final Score: SMU 22, Santa Clara 6, Record 1-0**

## Game Two – Missouri Tigers
**Attendance 35,000**
**10/4/1947, Cotton Bowl, Dallas, TX**

The first home game of the year was played in the Cotton Bowl against the University of Missouri. The Ponies had defeated Missouri by the score of 17-0 in 1946. The 1947 Tigers had defeated a Saint Louis team 19-0 on September 20th but had a loss to Ohio State the following week 13-7. It was a slow first quarter with both teams being scoreless.

In the second quarter, the Mustangs picked up the pace on offense with a Walker pass to Bobby Folsom and the running of Ed Green and Walker. After scoring a touchdown and the extra point, the score was 7-0 Mustangs. The Mustangs went on to score three additional touchdowns, with Walker primarily passing to Parker for

*A lot of bodies in a dark picture of the 1947 SMU/Missouri Game*

| Statistics, SMU vs. Missouri | | |
|---|---|---|
| | **SMU** | **Missouri** |
| First Downs | 12 | 14 |
| Yards Rushing | 230 | 231 |
| Yards Passing | 71 | 75 |
| Pass Attempts | 11 | 15 |
| Pass Completes | 5 | 4 |
| Passes Intercepted | 0 | 2 |
| Fumbles Recovered | 3 | 1 |
| Punting Average | 40.5 | 35 |
| Yards Kick Returns | 151 | 177 |
| Yards Penalized | 5 | 20 |

scores and Walker adding the extra points.

The most memorable play from the Missouri game was what many have described as the greatest single run in Cotton Bowl history. Walker started an ordinary right sweep from his twenty-three-yard line. When he knew the run was going nowhere, Walker reversed field going back to the left. Several Missouri defenders caught up with him around the 50-yard line, but Walker reversed field again, cutting through many of the same Missouri defenders that he had gone through on his first cut-back. Then with a sudden burst of speed, Walker charged down the sideline until he ran out of bounds at his 20-yard line. The *Dallas Morning News* described Walker's run as "one of the most brilliant runs the old Cotton Bowl has ever seen."

Once again, the statistics of the game indicate how close a football game the 1947 Missouri/SMU game was.

In explaining Missouri's loss, a *Dallas Morning News* article stated," But they (Missouri) just didn't have a rocket to let loose, and the Mustangs did — the man Walker."

**Final Score: SMU 35, Missouri 19, Record 2-0**

## Game Three – Oklahoma A&M Aggies
**Attendance 18,000**
**10/11/1947, Lewis Field, Stillwater, OK**

The Oklahoma A&M/SMU game was played on dedication Saturday of the new A&M football field in Stillwater, Oklahoma. The Aggies, which later became the Cowboys, had a 2-1 record at the time they played the Mustangs. The Farmers had beaten Kansas State 12-0 in their opener and followed that with a 14-7 victory over TCU. A loss followed the next week to Denver by the score of 26-14.

Unlike earlier games in the year, the Ponies scored in the first quarter; primarily on the passing of Doak Walker to take an early 7-0 lead. Early in the second quarter through a good defensive play by Sid Halliday, the Mustangs recovered a fumble on the Aggie 21-yard line. Carries by McKissack and Green, plus passing by Walker, resulted in a touchdown score by Walker from the 2-yard line. Near the end of the second quarter, Frank Payne had an interception to stall an Aggie drive. With passing by Gilbert Johnson and several short runs by Moxley; the Ponies made it 21-0 at halftime. The second half was primarily the Aggies' game, with A&M scoring against the Mustang reserves in the third quarter. The fourth quarter was a back-and-forth contest. However, the biggest play of the game occurred when Walker had a 66-yard quick kick

*Ed Green carries runs against the Okie Aggies on a sweep*

| Statistics, SMU vs. Oklahoma A&M | | |
|---|---|---|
|  | SMU | Oklahoma A&M |
| First Downs | 10 | 13 |
| Yards Rushing | 115 | 13 |
| Yards Passing | 88 | 13 |
| Pass Attempts | 17 | 11 |
| Pass Completes | 9 | 2 |
| Passes Intercepted | 1 | 0 |
| Fumbles Recovered | 1 | 2 |
| Punting Average | 43.2 | 28.2 |
| Number of Penalties | 7 | 6 |

on a third-down play. The kick was picked up by Aggie Spavitol, who would have scored on the return if it had not been for a touchdown-saving tackle by Walker on the SMU 14-yard line. On the next play, a fumble on an A&M running play resulted in the second A&M score as an A&M guard recovered the ball in the end-zone.

The final score reflects another close SMU game, but the Ponies generated a lot more offense than the Aggies.

**Final Score: SMU 21, Oklahoma A&M 14, Record 3-0**

## Game Four – Rice Institute Owls #15
**Attendance 23,000**
**10/18/1947, Ownby Stadium, University Park, TX**

The Rice game was the Mustang's first game of the season against a ranked opponent. In the 1940s and 1950s, the Owls played competitive football and were always considered a tough opponent. In the 1946 game, the Owls had beaten the Mustangs 19-6, and the Owls were a co-favorite to win the Southwest Conference Championship in 1947. However, the Owls lost their opening game to Louisiana State 21-14 on September 27th but tied Southern California 7-7 the following week. The Owls earned their national ranking with a solid 33-0 victory over Tulane on October 11th in the third game of the 1947 season.

*Students carrying their torches to burn "Sammy the Owl."*

The biggest yell practice of the season, which also included a parade, was held the night before the Rice game. The "Blue Shirts" were out in force, and their presence always raised the spirit level at yell practices and home games since the Shirts included approximately 70 men. After the yell practice, there was a touch light parade along the drag that ended with the burning of an effigy of "Sammy" the Rice Owl. In the *SMU Campus* Patterson, head cheerleader urged everyone to bring their torches. The yell leaders provided the fire.

Rice was the first team of the 1947 season the Mustangs faced that ran a T-Formation offense. Rice quarterback, Virgil Eikenberg, was considered a better ball handler in the T-formation than the legendary Longhorn T-quarterback Bobby Layne. The Fighting Birds also had a seasoned backfield to complement Eikenberg. As co-champions of the Southwest Conference of 1946, the Owls also had a veteran line with two capable pass receivers by the last name of Williams — Froggie and Windell. For SMU to shut out the Ricemen was a major accomplishment and not an easy task. The *Dallas Morning News* noted the defensive efforts of SMU lineman Lewis, Cook, Ethridge, and Hamberger.

The statistics of the game are listed on page 115.

| Statistics, SMU vs. Rice Institute | | |
|---|---|---|
| | **SMU** | **Rice Institute** |
| First Downs | 15 | 13 |
| Yards Rushing | 253 | 132 |
| Yards Passing | 71 | 121 |
| Pass Attempts | 9 | 23 |
| Pass Completes | 7 | 8 |
| Passes Intercepted | 3 | 0 |
| Fumbles Recovered | 3 | 2 |
| Punting Average | 33.7 | 42 |
| Yards Penalized | 20 | 10 |

*An Owl tackles Walker after catching a pass*

As mentioned earlier, Rice was one a co-favorite to win the Southwest Conference in 1947. Being from Houston, Tasos Pappadas, one of the SMU cheerleaders, noted that his Houston friend Joe Tusa had bragged before the game about how badly Rice was going to beat the Ponies. Tusa had little to say when the Mustangs not only beat Rice but delivered a shutout to the Owls.

Although it was early in the season, the SMU fans knew that the 1947 season could be a special one for the lads of SMU.

**Final Score: SMU 14, Rice Owls 0, Record 4-0**

## Game Five – UCLA Bruins #16
**Attendance 64,197**
**10/25/1947, Los Angeles Memorial Coliseum, Los Angeles, CA**

The 1947 UCLA game was the second Mustang game on the west coast and the second game against a ranked team. Travel for this game was a lot different than travel to the Santa Clara game, as the football team flew. In addition, SMU's seventy-five-member band traveled to the West Coast by train. Head cheerleader,

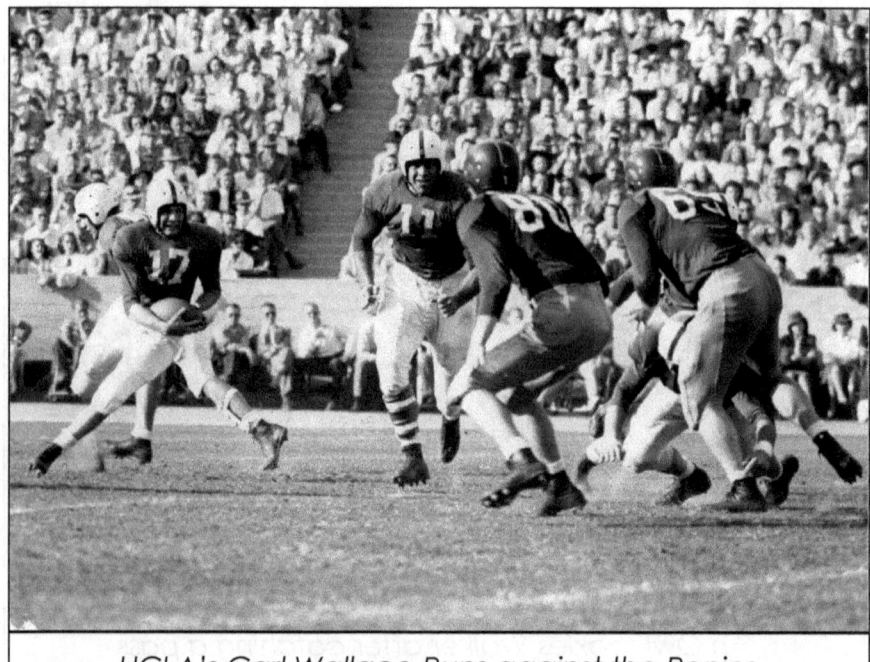

UCLA's Carl Wallace Runs against the Ponies

Joe Patterson, even convinced SMU President Umphrey Lee to give him $50 so Peruna could travel to Los Angeles on the train with the SMU band and cheerleaders. The night before the game, a Los Angeles cab driver was a little taken aback when he drove a miniature horse in the backseat of his cab from the train station to the hotel. Unfortunately, the cab driver did not receive an extra tip because of Peruna's limited travel budget.

On game day, the SMU band was on the radio for thirty minutes before the game playing numerous jazz tunes, and after the game, the SMU band toured the ABC, NBC, and CBS studios and visited Hollywood for a short tour of the homes of several movie stars.

When asked for a comment before the UCLA game, Coach Matty Bell said only, "We'll play 'em a good ball game." UCLA had only lost one game prior to SMU which was the week earlier when Northwestern beat the Bruins in an upset 27-26. The Bruins had a 26-0 lead only to have the Wildcats come back to score 27 straight points for the victory. UCLA was expected to go to the Rose Bowl before they played SMU but the loss to Northwestern was a sign of a downhill season, and the Bruins finished the 1947 season 4-5 and did not go to a 1948 bowl game.

The SMU/UCLA game was the lowest scoring SMU game of the 1947 football season. As indicated by the score, the game was a defensive struggle. The game was scoreless until the fourth quarter. In the last quarter, Matty Bell changed the offensive approach by sending Gil Johnson into the backfield to shift the Mustangs to more of a pass-oriented game. On his first play of the game, Johnson passed to Paul Page, who took the ball to the UCLA 2-yard line. After a couple of running plays that netted the Mustangs only a yard, Walker went in for a score and kicked the extra point to give the Mustangs a 7-0 lead. UCLA had moved the ball well on offense most of the game but had fumbled twice inside the Pony ten-yard line. SMU also had chances to score as in the first half, and the Mustangs had advanced to the Bruin's two-yard line. SMU tried to punch the ball over with multiple dives by numerous backfield players but could not score before time expired at the half. Even the opening kickoff provided SMU excitement, with Page Paul returning the kickoff 49 yards, but the UCLA defense stiffened and the Mustang's drive soon died out.

| Statistics, SMU vs. UCLA | | |
|---|---|---|
|  | **SMU** | **UCLA** |
| First Downs | 7 | 13 |
| Yards Rushing | 116 | 153 |
| Yards Passing | 103 | 95 |
| Pass Attempts | 6 | 20 |
| Pass Completes | 3 | 7 |
| Passes Intercepted | 3 | 1 |
| Fumbles Recovered | 3 | 0 |
| Punting Average | 33 | 30 |
| Yards Penalized | 24 | 40 |

With six turnovers during the game by the Bruins, the Mustangs didn't need much scoring to pull off a victory.

Approximately 700 Mustang fans had attended the game in Los Angeles. Also, the *Dallas Morning News* reported that the redshirted Mustang Men's Male Chorus had carried the SMU team off the field at the end of the game. The Mustang Chorus included about 113 members, but not all had made the trip to Los Angeles.

The Mustangs continued to entertain after the game, as the Mustang Band played numerous jazz hits as well as singing tunes like "Carry Harry to the Ferry," "Hullabaloo," and "Drunk Last Night." The *SMU Campus* reported in the October 29, 1947, edition:

> As darkness descended on the massive concrete and steel stadium the band followed by the Mustang men, and hundreds of rooters and well-wishers, marched up the ramp and out of the stadium and turned down Menlo Street. The fans were last seen headed in the direction of downtown LA.

**Final Score: SMU 7, UCLA 0, Record 5-0**

# Game Six - University of Texas #3
Attendance 50,000
11/1/1947, Cotton Bowl, Dallas, TX

The 1947 SMU/University of Texas game was one of the biggest college football matchups of the 1947 college season. The Longhorns were ranked No. 3 and the Ponies were ranked No. 8. SMU had a seven-game losing streak against the Orange Bloods going into the 1947 game. At game time, both teams were undefeated, and both teams had minor injuries to their respective key players. Since the game was played in the Cotton Bowl, the Mustangs had the home field advantage, but the Longhorns always had a large following of tea sips, particularly when the game is played in Dallas and especially when the game is in the Cotton Bowl. The rivalry between the two schools in 1947 was not at the same level of animosity that developed between the school's years later. A dance was held the night before the game in the SMU Student Union Building for students from both universities. Texas students came to the Round-Up dance via an invite in The Daily Texan earlier in the week. The single-ticket price to the dance was a breathtaking fifty cents.

The Texas game opened with one of the most historic kickoff returns in SMU football history. Taking the Texas kickoff, Frank Payne took the ball to the ten-yard line. With the ball partially hidden on his hip, Payne then handed off to Paul Page, who streaked down the sidelines an additional seventy-one yards. The first play of the game changed the tone of the entire 1947 SMU/Texas game. Facing a fourth down, Walker completed a pass to McKissack on the four-yard line for a first down. With two-line plunges and no success, Walker faked a line plunge and handed off to Paul Page who scampered in for the score. Only two and half minutes had elapsed on the clock, and with Walker's extra point it was SMU 7-0.

Harry Taylor, who was the head linesman at the 1947 TEXAS/SMU game, asked an audience at the Frog Hotel Texas Quarterback Club two questions the following Monday. The first question: How many had attended the game that Saturday? About 30 hands went up. Second question: How many had seen the handoff on the opening kickoff? Not one person raised their hand.

An article in the Ft. Worth Star-Telegram provided details on the trickery of the handoff play.

## SPORTS
### Like Longhorns, Fans Also Slip on Hand-Off

**BY LORIN McMULLEN**
Star-Telegram Sports Writer.

Harry Taylor, who was head linesman in the Southern Methodist-University of Texas game, brought out an interesting point about the classic Monday at the Frog Club's Hotel Texas quarterback session.

Taylor asked for a show of hands by those who had seen the game. About 30 men raised arms. Then he asked:

"How many saw the hand-off (Frank Payne to Paul Page) on the opening kickoff?"

Not one spectator claimed to have seen it.

The official then commented that this indicated the Mustangs' perfection in executing the play, which he rated highlight of the game.

Taylor had a perfect view of the maneuver from his station on the east side of the field. Payne, he said, backed well into the end zone to take the long kick, then tucked the ball on his right side and partially behind him in full view of approaching Longhorns on his right side, but screened completely from those on his left side of the field, which the Mustangs wished to have cleared for Page.

The Texas players were drawn over. Taylor said it did not occur to him that "something was up" until he noticed that Payne was moving at about three-quarter speed, rather than the full-steam-ahead he'd have employed had it been a conventional run-back. And about that time, Taylor said, Page whizzed past, took the ball and headed up field.

FRANK PAYNE.

* * *

*Details on the trickery of the handoff play*

The only SMU kickoff play that comes close to the perfection of this planned play was "the Miracle on Fourth Street" in 1982. With the score tied 27-27 and only 17 seconds on the clock, Blane Smith purposely mishandled the Texas Tech kickoff on the ten-yard line and threw the ball back to Bobby Leach who streaked 91 yards for the winning SMU touchdown.

In the second quarter, even a Doak Walker interception couldn't stop the Longhorns from scoring. Three superb passes by Layne put the ball on the SMU thirteen yard line, and then Canaday carried

| Statistics, SMU vs. Texas | | |
|---|---|---|
| | SMU | Texas |
| First Downs | 7 | 9 |
| Yards Rushing | 108 | 76 |
| Yards Passing | 91 | 120 |
| Pass Attempts | 7 | 15 |
| Pass Completes | 4 | 9 |
| Passes Intercepted | 1 | 0 |
| Fumbles Recovered | 2 | 1 |
| Punting Average | 39.5 | 51.8 |
| Yards Penalized | 15 | 10 |

McKissack, Walker, and Reinking enjoy the victory over Texas

to the SMU four-yard line. After a first down, Tom Landry carried the pigskin in for a score, and Guess kicked the extra point for the 7-7 tie.

To change up things for this big game, Matty Bell used Johnson and Walker in the same backfield for the first time in the 1947 season. In the second quarter, Johnson came into the game as a tailback and completed a long pass to Walker, who was then playing fullback. McKissack carried in for the score, and Walker added the extra point to make it 14-7.

The Steers final touchdown came on a drive late in the third quarter that started from the Texas 29-yard line. Bobby Layne passing got the Longhorns to the SMU twenty-two-yard line as the fourth quarter began. A couple of Texas interior runs gained little, but then Layne passed to Gillory for a score. With Guess kicking the extra point into a strong wind, the extra point failed. The statistics for the game were equally close.

The long-awaited battle between two former Highland Park high school stars ended as close as their friendship, and by the margin of a single extra point, the Ponies had prevailed.

**Final Score: SMU 14, Texas 13, Record 6-0**

## Game Seven – Texas A&M Aggies
**Attendance 28,000**
**11/8/1947, Kyle Field, College Station, TX**

Founded in 1876, Texas A&M was an all-male school, and in 1947 all the students were members of the Corps of Cadets. For many years, Texas A&M was nicknamed "Sing-Sing on the Brazos." That moniker went away when women were admitted in 1963, and Texas A&M had a sudden explosion in student enrollment. Before female students attended Texas A&M, a male student had to have a strong reason to go to A&M or desire for one of a short list of majors that included being an engineer, a farmer or rancher, or serving in the military. Even fifty years later, the Corps of Cadets is not for everyone. It might be a record but Tyler Gillespie, a Lake Highlands high school freshman, was in the Texas A&M Corps for a half a day before transferring to Baylor. The biggest thrill at any A&M football game for a non-Aggie is witnessing the Fightin' Texas Aggie Band at half-time. The Aggie Band is one of the unique half-time experiences in American college football.

Before the game, a headline article in the November 6 *SMU Campus* titled, "Rally Tonight to Hang Mock Aggie" used non-politically correct words, which read:

> Head cheerleader Joe Patterson has announced the formation of a gigantic pep rally Thursday night in front of McFarlin Auditorium at 6:45 p.m. A march up the drag will climax by the hanging of an Aggie from the flagpole in the back of Perkins Hall.

Patterson also stated in the *SMU Campus* article that SMU had not beaten A&M in football since 1939 and closed his interview with "Git'em Mustangs!" Conference games were always tough throughout the history of the Southwest Conference. However, the A&M Farmers were only a .500 team when they played SMU in early November 1947. A&M's record was 3-3-1 at the time of the SMU game. In Southwest Conference play, the Aggies had beaten Baylor, lost to TCU, and tied Arkansas. A&M ran a double-wing offense, whereas SMU's previous opponents all had run a T formation.

*Halliday Tackles an Aggie Runner*

| Statistics, SMU vs. Texas A&M | | |
|---|---|---|
| | SMU | Texas A&M |
| First Downs | 15 | 6 |
| Yards Rushing | 131 | 13 |
| Yards Passing | 177 | 179 |
| Pass Attempts | 18 | 27 |
| Pass Completes | 16 | 11 |
| Passes Intercepted | 5 | 0 |
| Fumbles Recovered | 1 | 2 |
| Punting Average | 28.6 | 44.5 |
| Yards Penalized | 30 | 25 |

 The football conditions were ideal at Kyle Field in College Station that November Saturday day. Passing was the SMU emphasis in the A&M game, and passing strategy won the day for the Mustangs. Gilbert Johnson completed fourteen of sixteen passes, and Doak Walker added two more completions as Walker was two for two in passing. Johnson's passing to Paul Page led to a nine-play drive that resulted in a Paul Page touchdown catch. With Walker's extra point, the score was 7-0 at half-time. A Paul Page interception of an Aggie pass in the end zone in the third quarter halted the only serious Aggie scoring threat during the game. In total, the Mustangs had five interceptions for the game, two by Page and three by Reinking. In the fourth quarter, Raleigh Blakley caught a short pass from Johnson and scored on the short run after the catch. Frank Payne, with a fresh pair of legs, replaced Walker.

 Walker had played the first 54 minutes of the game playing both ways. Payne had several good carries that fueled a touchdown drive. Maybe it was the effect of a bad cold or a bad ankle or just being out of the game before the SMU touchdown, but Walker's kicking rhythm was off. Doak missed the extra point after the score. This miss broke Doak's string of 14 consecutive extra points after touchdowns. The final score 13-0 stood for the rest of the game.

**Final Score: SMU 13, Texas A&M 0, SMU Record 7-0**

Joe Redwine Patterson told me a side story to the 1947 SMU/A&M game. The story goes that A&M cadets in the Aggie Band charged the SMU football team in their effort to get off the football field after their half-time presentation. Patterson claimed that the SMU football team defended itself with the swinging of helmets and fists to fend off the hard-charging heavily instrumented Aggies. For years, I questioned the validity of the story as every 1947 SMU alumni that I had spoken to or met had no recollection of the halftime event ever happening.

However, the following letter appeared in the *SMU Campus* on November 19, 1947:

---

November 10, 1947

Mr. Madison Bell
Director of Athletics
Southern Methodist University
Dallas, Texas

Dear Mr. Bell:
We regret that during last Saturday's game some of the cadets ran through your team in their hurry to get off the field. We want you to know that it was entirely unintentional and probably would not have happened if the band had not performed over time.

We understand that in a rush the team's physician had his glasses broken. If so, please notify us of the cost, the student body will be more than happy to replace them.

We are very sorry that this incident happened and we will try to prevent any such reoccurrence in the future.

Very truly yours,

William L. Brown
Cadet Colonel of the Corp
A.D. Bruce, Jr.
President, Student Senate

## Game Eight – University of Arkansas
**Attendance 23,000**
**11/15/1947, Ownby Stadium, University Park, TX**

The Razorbacks came into the SMU game with a respectable record of 4-3-1. Arkansas had started the season fast with three straight wins but then lost to both Baylor and Texas. The Razorbacks bounced back with a win over Mississippi 19-14, but then tied Texas A&M and lost 26-0 to Rice. Matty Bell made his typical comment regarding opposing teams before the Arkansas game. "There'd better not be any let-up against Arkansas, or we won't win," commented moanin' Matty. Arkansas had a couple of capable backs, including Clyde (Smackdown) Scott and the ever-dangerous Leon (Muscles) Campbell, who was known affectionately as the "human battering ram." At the time of the game, Scott was the leading rusher in the Southwest Conference. Walker had recovered from his cold and his ankle injury was better, but not completely healed.

Just sixty seconds into the game, the fans knew that this was not going to be the average ho-hum SMU home football game. A male fan charged onto the playing field and started cussing at referee Jack Sisco. The confrontation quickly escalated into the throwing of punches by both individuals. The end results were that Referee Sisco left the field for medical attention. The police forcibly removed the fan from the field.

The first line in Felix R. McKnight's *Dallas Morning News* article on the SMU/Arkansas game said: "On to glory drove Southern Methodist's unbeaten Mustangs Saturday." The game didn't start out with much glory, however, as the Mustangs fell behind for the first game of the 1947 season. The *Dallas Morning News* noted that in the first quarter the Ponies appeared to be dull and uninspired.

McKnight also described the Razorbacks' Scott's running in the first quarter as "Scott's cannon-shot spurts through wazon-size holes in the middle of the line." Clyde Scott was named an All-American running back in 1948. Of note, Doak Walker was named an All-American quarterback that same year.

The only Arkansas score was the result of a low snap from center that forced SMU punter Ed Green to run and not punt. Green ended up on the SMU thirty-one-yard line. It was one-yard short of a first down. It only took three plays with the primary running of

| Statistics, SMU vs. Arkansas | | |
|---|---|---|
| | SMU | Arkansas |
| First Downs | 18 | 10 |
| Yards Rushing | 200 | 91 |
| Yards Passing | 106 | 54 |
| Pass Attempts | 18 | 9 |
| Pass Completes | 9 | 3 |
| Passes Intercepted | 0 | 3 |
| Fumbles Recovered | 2 | 1 |
| Punting Average | 32.8 | 41.4 |
| Yards Penalized | 45 | 81 |

Campbell for the Hogs to score. The extra point by Arkansas kicker Duval Thornton was wide, and the score was 6-0 Arkansas.

Shocked by the Hogs' score, the Mustangs came right back with an 81-yard drive in the second quarter. The sharp passing of Gilbert Johnson and the running of

Doak Walker and McKissack lead to a Mustang touchdown. Walker added the extra point, and the Ponies led 7-6. The score remained that way until the fourth quarter when Dick McKissack recovered an Arkansas fumble. A pass from Doak Walker took the Ponies to the two-yard-line where Walker scored off tackle. With the extra point, the score was 14-6 Mustangs, which was how the contest ended.

The statistics of the game reflect the skill of the Mustang backfield. Doak Walker, Paul Page, Dick McKissack, and Gilbert Johnson accounted for 306 yards of total offense. Walker was limited in his running because of a bad ankle, but McKissack had ninety yards on twenty-two carries, and Paul Page picked up sixty-two yards on eleven carries.

The Razorbacks hurt themselves with critical penalties especially during the fourth quarter of the game. An illegal use of the hands brought a halt to one drive with a fifteen-yard penalty. Also, referee Sisco ejected Arkansas guard Ray Peters in the fourth quarter for pulverizing center Cecil Sutphin to the ground before the

*Walker running wide against the Porkers*

snap. Arkansas also lost Clyde Scott for the remainder of the game when Scott dove into Peruna's sideline pen while trying to catch a pass. Scott had sixty-five yards rushing on twelve carries.

**Final Score: SMU 14, Arkansas 6, SMU Record 8-0**

## Game Nine – Baylor University Bears
**Attendance 12,000**
**11/22/1947, Municipal Stadium, Waco, TX**

At Waco's Municipal Stadium, the Baylor/SMU game was played in the rain, wind, and mud. The rain fell primarily before the game started, and this early rain made the fifty yards in the middle of the field into one huge mud pit. For fifty-six minutes, the two teams battled to a 0-0 tie. Interceptions and fumbles were major factors contributing to the game being scoreless that late. The mud and the cold were the biggest factors contributing to slips, lack of traction, and not being able to throw a dry football.

Because of artificial turf, many college football players today have not played a college game on natural turf. With indoor practice facilities at most Division I-A schools, players also may never have even practiced in the mud and the rain at the college level. Currently, SMU is one of the few Division I colleges that does not have an indoor practice facility. The author fondly remembers

*Cook hits a Bear that is launched through the air*

building horns of mud on top of his helmet in junior high school while practicing during a heavy rainstorm. There was no greater joy than smashing into the equally horned opposing line or tackling a player with a helmet covered in mud. Oh, the forgotten joy of playing organized football in the mud.

The scoreless game was broken with approximately four minutes to play in the game when Walker kicked a field goal, making the score 3-0. Walker's field goal was the first field goal kicked in the Southwest Conference in the 1947 season. The field goal barely made it over the crossbar. Scoring a field goal must have inspired the Ponies because Paul Page came up with an interception on the ensuing Baylor drive, and returned the ball to mid-field. Page and Walker led a fifty-yard drive that ended with Page taking a flea-flicker handoff on the left side of the line to score the game's only touchdown with only 3.5 seconds left on the clock. The press noted that in making a mass player substitution late in the game, Matty Bell had sent ten perfectly clean uniforms into the game in total disregard for uniform cleaning bills. The statistics of the game are listed on page 130.

Not only had the Ponies won, but they also had accomplished their first goal of the season — the SMU Mustangs were going to the 1948 Cotton Bowl.

**Final Score: SMU 10, Baylor 0, SMU Record 9-0**

| Statistics, SMU vs. Baylor | | |
|---|---|---|
|  | SMU | Baylor |
| First Downs | 14 | 4 |
| Yards Rushing | 140 | 72 |
| Yards Passing | 12 | 0 |
| Pass Attempts | 6 | 4 |
| Pass Completes | 1 | 0 |
| Passes Intercepted | 1 | 0 |
| Fumbles Recovered | 2 | 2 |
| Punting Average | 35.8 | 38.4 |
| Yards Penalized | 5 | 50 |

## Game Ten – Texas Christian University
Attendance 31,000
11/29/1947, Amon G. Carter Stadium, Fort Worth, TX

Just as in 2016, in 1947 SMU's biggest football rival was Texas Christian University in Fort Worth, Texas. In 1935, both teams had claimed to be the national champion of college football. Sports writer Grantland Rice had described the "Game of the Century" as follows:

> In a TCU Stadium that seated 30,000 spectators, over 36,000 wildly excited Texans and visitors every corner of the map packed, jammed, and fought their way into every square foot of standing and seating space to see one of the greatest football games ever played ... as this tense, keyed up the crowd even leaped the wire fences from the top of automobiles....

The 1935 SMU/TCU game ended with a 20-14 victory for the Mustangs. However, SMU went on to lose to Sanford in the Rose Bowl 7-0. The Toads beat LSU in the Sugar Bowl 3-2 in a muddy Tulane Stadium. The college football poll system awarded numerous national champions in 1935 besides SMU and TCU.

Paul Page running with John Hamberger blocking against TCU

Other polls awarded the championship to the University of Minnesota, Princeton University, and even a co-championship gave to TCU/LSU.

In 1946, the student councils of the two universities added a prize to be awarded to the winner of the annual SMU/TCU game – a skillet. The skillet name came from the idea behind the Michigan/Wisconsin award of the "Little Brown Jug." Through the years, "the skillet" became known as the "Iron Skillet."

As usual, Matty Bell predicted a hard game for the Ponies. Being undefeated and already chosen to play in the Cotton Bowl in January 1948, the Ponies were the odds-on favorites to go 10-0 for the season. TCU had a 4-4-1 season record entering the late November game with the Mustangs, but the Froggies had been held scoreless against Kansas, Texas, Arkansas, and Rice.

Also, as usual, head cheerleader Patterson urged the Pony faithful to attend two yell practices — Friday night at 6:30 at McFarlin Auditorium and Saturday at noon in front of the Texas Hotel in downtown Fort Worth. Patterson was quoted by the *SMU Campus* as saying, "It is the TCU homecoming, and they will be out for

| Statistics, SMU vs. TCU | | |
|---|---|---|
| | SMU | TCU |
| First Downs | 13 | 7 |
| Yards Rushing | 151 | 53 |
| Yards Passing | 279 | 156 |
| Pass Attempts | 24 | 12 |
| Pass Completes | 13 | 9 |
| Passes Intercepted | 2 | 1 |
| Fumbles Recovered | 0 | 2 |
| Punting Average | 37.5 | 42.0 |
| Yards Penalized | 5 | 30 |

blood. The school has shown good spirit all year, and even though this is the last game of the season, it is not the time to let down." Patterson also made a vague reference to the "twelfth man" being at all the games and ended with this quote: "Let's be out to gig the Frogs." Patterson seemed to have caught a little of the Spirit of Aggieland in making his statement.

The first quarter of the game was all TCU. The Frogs were the first team to score and the score came the second time TCU got the ball. Marching from mid-field in six plays the Toads scored on a two-yard run by fullback Pete Stout. Later in the first quarter, TCU's Berry intercepted a Gil Johnson pass and raced all the way to the SMU nine-yard line. Four plays later, Stout scored again on a two-yard plunge. With a blocked extra point, the score was 12-0 Frogs.

The statistics of the game indicate a lot of SMU offense, but most of that offense came late in the game.

Walker's performance in the SMU/TCU game led to his being named to the College Football All-American team by having three long kickoff returns, making several long runs from scrimmage, completing 10 out of 14 passes, playing extremely well on defense, and bringing the Mustangs from behind in the final seconds of play. Walker had 475 total yards against TCU in the 1947 game. John Hamberger was correct. The 1947 SMU Mustangs were a slightly

*Walker in SMU/TCU game*

above-average team, but they had one player who led the team to 1947 football glory. His name was Ewell Doak Walker, and he was one of the greatest college football players who ever lived.

**Final Score: SMU 19, TCU 19, SMU Record 9-0-1**

## Recap of the Regular 1947 SMU Football Season

At the end of the regular 1947 season, the Mustangs had accomplished the goals the football team had set after their first fall practice in1947. The team had gone undefeated and the team was going to the Cotton Bowl. In the Southwest Conference standings, the Ponies finished first, but both Texas and Rice had scored more points during the regular season. Even last-place Texas A&M had scored the same number of points as SMU. Both Texas and Rice had held their opponents to fewer points scored during the season.

A recap of the SMU 1947 season shows how close statistically the Mustang team was to its opponents in the ten-game season.

| 1947 Final Southwest Conference Standings ||||||
|---|---|---|---|---|---|
| Team | W | L | T | Pts | Ops |
| SMU | 9 | 0 | 1 | 169 | 77 |
| Texas | 9 | 1 | 0 | 265 | 67 |
| Rice | 6 | 3 | 1 | 202 | 74 |
| Arkansas | 5 | 4 | 1 | 170 | 176 |
| Baylor | 5 | 5 | 0 | 128 | 138 |
| TCU | 4 | 4 | 1 | 105 | 86 |
| Texas A&M | 3 | 6 | 1 | 169 | 185 |

| Statistics, SMU vs. 1947 Opponents |||
|---|---|---|
| | SMU | Opponents |
| First Downs | 120 | 101 |
| Yards Rushing | 1,627 | 1,044 |
| Yards Passing | 1,016 | 830 |
| Pass Attempts | 134 | 157 |
| Pass Completes | 75 | 62 |
| Passes Intercepted | 19 | 9 |
| Fumbles Recovered | 18 | 13 |
| Punting Average | 37.1 | 37.7 |
| Yards Penalized | 238 | 329 |

If ESPN had existed in 1947, ESPN should have done a "30 for 30" segment on the SMU Mustang football team. At the beginning of the season, SMU was an underdog and projected to finish about fourth in the Southwest Conference. Although SMU shut out four opponents, the team also won by fourteen points or less in seven of their ten games.

To show how different the game of college football has become over seventy years, consider the individual offensive statistics from the 2015 season listed on page 135.

| Offensive Statistics, 2015 |||
|---|---|---|
| Individual | School | Single Season Record |
| Brandon Doughty | Western Kentucky | 5,055 yards passing |
| Derrick Henry | Alabama | 2,219 yards rushing |
| Keyarris Garrett | Tulsa | 1,588 yards receiving |
| Johnny Townsend | Florida | 45.4 punting average |
| Chris Callahan | Baylor | 83 of 83 extra points |

The Mustangs total offense for the 1947 season looks anemic compared to the high scoring offenses of today. The Ponies only had twenty-four touchdowns for the season, and Doak Walker kicked only two field goals. Still, the Ponies outscored their regular season opponents 169-77.

The winning difference in the 1947 season was the play of Doak Walker. Walker's statistics for the 1947 season are impressive, even by today's standards.

- 684 yards rushing on 163 carries and eleven touchdowns
- Kicked 18 of 22 extra points
- Returned 20 punts for 256 yards
- Returned 10 kickoffs for a 38.7-yard average
- Returned 20 punts for 256 yards
- Completed 29 of 51 passes for 342 yards
- Caught eight passes for 132 yards
- Punted for a 33-yard average

An illustration of how his fellow SMU athletes admired Doak Walker is the story of Walker joining the SMU basketball team after the 1947 season. In one basketball game, he was sent into the game with only 30 seconds to play. Although Walker never touched the ball for those 30 seconds, his basketball teammates carried him off the court on their shoulders. His teammates explained that they "just wanted to make a big football star feel at home."

*A sold-out Cotton Bowl for the 1947 SMU/Texas Game*

## One Missed Texas Extra Point Could Have Been the Difference

Kicking into a strong wind, in the SMU/Texas game, the Texas second extra point failed. A missed extra point allowed the Ponies to escape a possible tie against the Texas Longhorns to win 14-13. If the two teams had tied and all the other 1947 Southwest Conference games had the same results, Texas would have gone to the Cotton Bowl instead of SMU. But again, as Dandy Don Meredith said many times in the NFL announcing booth, "If 'ifs' and 'buts' were candy and nuts, we'd all have a Merry Christmas."

## Dallas Support of the Mustangs

The Ponies of the late 1940s and early 1950s received great support from the football fans of Dallas. Doak Walker sparked SMU fan support like no time in the history of SMU football.

# Chapter Ten
# 1948 Cotton Bowl

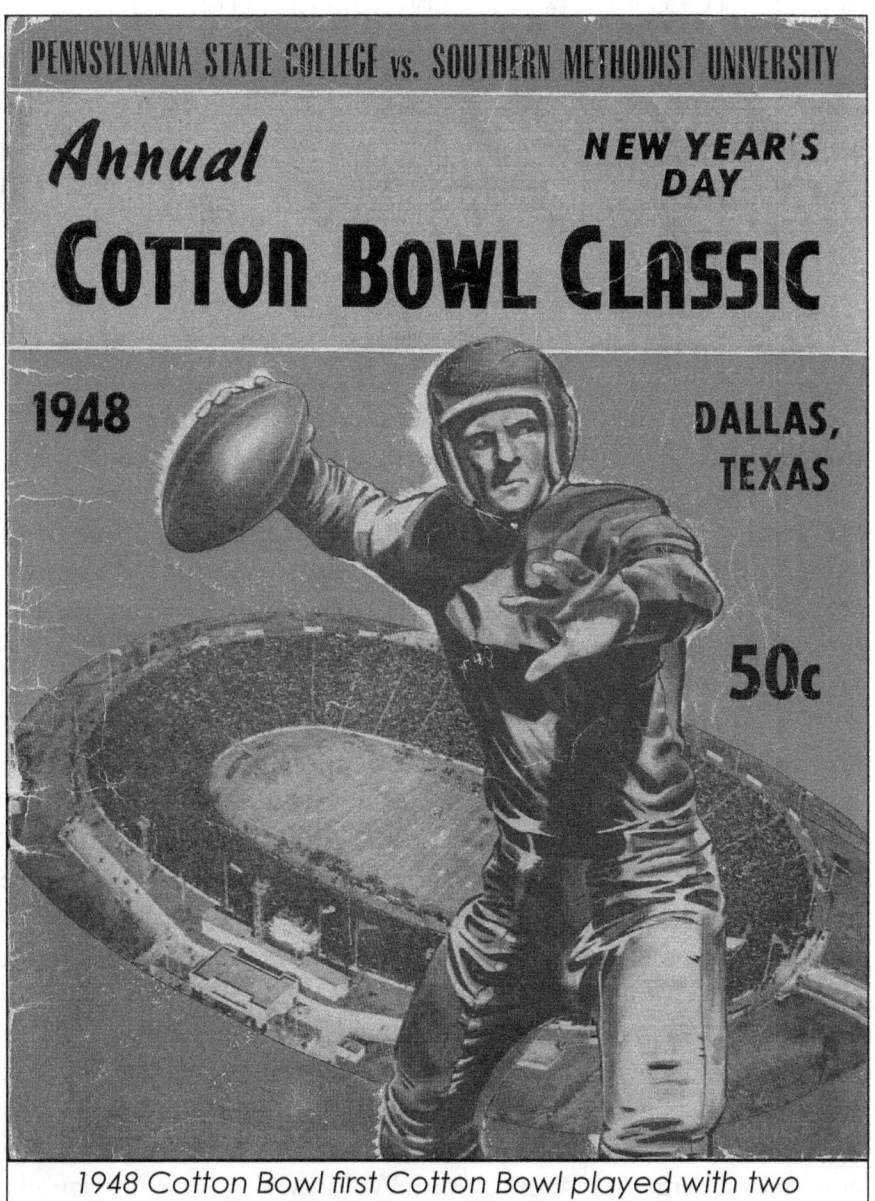

1948 Cotton Bowl first Cotton Bowl played with two undefeated teams

| 1947 Regular Season Records: SMU and Penn State ||||
|---|---|---|---|
| SMU 22 | Santa Clara 7 | Penn State 27 | Wash. State 6 |
| SMU 35 | Missouri 19 | Penn State 54 | Bucknell 0 |
| SMU 21 | Okla A&M 14 | Penn State 75 | Fordham 0 |
| SMU 14 | Rice 0 | Penn State 40 | Syracuse 0 |
| SMU 7 | UCLA 0 | Penn State 21 | W. Virginia 14 |
| SMU 14 | Texas 13 | Penn State 46 | Colgate 0 |
| SMU 13 | Texas A&M 0 | Penn State 7 | Temple 0 |
| SMU 14 | Arkansas 6 | Penn State 20 | Navy 7 |
| SMU 10 | Baylor 0 | Penn State 29 | Pittsburgh 0 |
| SMU 19 | TCU 19 | | |

The Cotton Bowl in Dallas, Texas, was the newer version of the old Dixie Bowl that was located at Dallas Fair Park. The first Cotton Bowl game in 1937 drew approximately 16,000 fans to see the game between TCU and Marquette. The 1948 Cotton Bowl game, the 12th Cotton Bowl game, could have attracted a crowd of 100,000 if the seats had been available. With a seating capacity of 45,507, more than 90,000 applications were received for the reserved seats, which cost $4.40 per ticket.

For the first time in the bowl's history, the game featured two undefeated teams. SMU (9-0-1) was ranked No. 3 and Penn State (9-0-0) was ranked No. 4 in the country. In 1947, the Lambert Trophy, which was emblematic of the Eastern Football Champion, was awarded to Penn State. The Lions also led the nation in defense in 1947, allowing only 76.7 yards per game and shutting out six of their nine opponents. The regular 1947 season was impressive for both teams.

The two teams also were evenly matched weight wise. SMU's starting line averaged 207 pounds while Penn State's starting line averaged 203 pounds. The biggest position weight discrepancy was with the centers, with SMU's center Cecil Sutphin weighing 175 pounds and Penn State's center, John Wolosky, weighing 205 pounds. Matty Bell decided to play SMU's backup center Lloyd Berker (195 pounds) for a good portion of the game to help add more weight to the SMU line. The substitution of Berker didn't seem to help Sutphin, as he broke his leg near the end of the game. The other key matchup in the game was Penn State lineman, Steve Suhey, who many considered as the best college lineman in the country and Earl Cook, SMU's All-Southwest Conference guard. Dallas sporting goods company Cullum-Boren placed an ad in the *Dallas Morning News* that contained a cartoon of Cook blocking Suhey with the title "Consider Yo'Self as Blocked." Suhey also received press in The *Dallas Morning News* as he stepped off the train in Dallas after a long trip from the East Coast and made the following comment after receiving his traditional Cotton Bowl 10-gallon hat: "Now all we've got to do is convince somebody we've got a football team."

However, the bigger story surrounded the fact that Penn State had been rejected from other major bowl games in the south because Penn State had two black players on the squad — two-way back Wally Triplett and Dennie Hoggard, who were both juniors.

Before the game, SMU released several statements indicating the school's acceptance of playing Penn State, which had two black players. Matty Bell told the *Dallas Morning News*, "We have no objections ourselves; after all, we're supposed to live in a democracy." Sophomore backup tailback, Frank Payne Jr., also stated that the SMU team had no issues with facing the two black players. "When it first came up, they said, 'does anyone object?' Payne recalled, 'Nobody did, and that was the last I heard about it.'" Even fifty years later, Payne said the SMU players never gave the 1948 Cotton Bowl any thought about being a breakthrough racial event, "We didn't even think about it that way. They were just two other football players." Patty Bell Kendrick, Matty Bell's daughter, also said sixty-eight years after the Cotton Bowl that Bell's experience of coaching at Haskell Indian Institute in Kansas probably contributed to his accepting stance on race at the time of the 1948 Cotton Bowl.

Since Dallas hotels were segregated in 1947, it was unclear where the Penn State team would stay during their time in Dallas. At SMU's suggestion, the Penn State team was given the option to stay at the Dallas Naval Air Station in Grand Prairie. Penn State accepted. Having the Penn State team stay in barracks on a military base might have been a psychological advantage for the Mustangs. Before the game, one Penn State player said, "We just came from barracks, and they put us right back in. We jumped over the fence one time. Our morale was way off."

Both teams had practiced hard the week before the game, and both teams had player injuries that worried the head coaches. Penn State halfback John Chuckran suffered a bad hip injury in a hard scrimmage the Saturday before the game and did not play in the Cotton Bowl. Both co-captains for the Nittany Lions, John Potsklan, and John Nolan, saw limited practice because of less serious injuries. Nolan started the game at right tackle, but Potsklan was replaced as a starter by Ed Czekaj at right end. Potsklan had been experiencing neuralgia of the chest, and these chest pains restricted his amount of practice and game day play. Nittany Lions coach, Bob Higgins, commented to the *Dallas Morning News* on their injuries with the following statement, "All I ask for is the presence of Nolan and Potsklan in the lineup. We have a fine football club, and we didn't make the trip down here from Pennsylvania to take a licking. If these boys are ready — and I am hopeful that they will be — we'll give the Ponies a ball game."

On the Mustang team, injuries and bad colds affected numerous reserve players such as Claud Hill, Harold Clark, and Bill Moxley. In typical Matty Bell style, he told the *Dallas Morning News*, "No ball club wades through a nine-game schedule as Penn State did without having a great team. It should be a great game. I wouldn't offer a prediction as to the outcome, but the Mustangs have been forced to battle for every decision this season, and they are not going to let down. A victory means too much for the team and this section of the country."

The Cotton Bowl Optimist Club Luncheon was held Wednesday before the game at the Baker Hotel in downtown Dallas. Numerous dignitaries from both Penn State and SMU attended. Penn State ordered approximately one hundred tickets for the luncheon. Tickets to the public were $1.50 each and they were sold at Buddy DeBorde Cigar Store in the Liberty Bank Building.

There was also a social function the night before the game. Norma Peterson, Doak Walker's girlfriend at the time and later his first wife, noted that Walker being a "straight arrow" declined to

*Team Captains before Cotton Bowl Kickoff*

take her to the Cotton Bowl function. Walker went to bed early before the Cotton Bowl game to get as much sleep as he could. Peterson wanted to attend the function so asked head cheerleader, Joe Patterson, to escort her to the event.

At the time, it was customary to name a queen for bowl games. Penn State brought Janet Blair, a Paramount starlet and big band singer from Altoona, Pennsylvania, who was Miss Penn State for the game. The *SMU Campus* noted that Miss Blair was accompanied by her parents Mr. and Mrs. Fred B. Lafferty. SMU countered with a good-looking woman of its own —Elizabeth Ann Stollenwerck, who attended as Miss SMU. Miss Stollenwerck was the 1947 SMU Homecoming Queen, as well as an SMU *Rotunda* beauty. Her father had played football at SMU and at the time was coaching football at Grand Prairie High School.

The Mustang Band and a high school band from White Oak, Texas, were scheduled to perform at halftime at the 1948 Cotton Bowl. The Penn State Blue Blazer band was not able to make the trip to Dallas. There also was mentioned in the *SMU Campus* that the Mustang Band was going to perform a "horse trick," first performed in 1935. In reality, the "horse trick" involved having several SMU students wear horse costumes to give the appearance that they

*A little straw to keep SMU players and coaches warm*

were riding a horse. This performance only added to the conclusion that SMU's 1948 half-time Cotton Bowl performance was truly a lame act.

## The Game

New Year's Day 1948 was a cold, clear day in Dallas at the Cotton Bowl. Temperatures were in the high thirties to the low forties. Since there were no gas heaters on the sidelines, the players put their feet in bales of hay to keep them warm. SMU scored twice in the first half. The first score was on a 53-yard pass from Doak Walker to Paul Page in the first quarter, and the second score was on a two-yard run by Walker in the second quarter. Walker's two-yard run came after a twenty-yard gain by fullback Dick McKissack. Walker had made the first extra point but was wide right on the second try. Walker had two chances for the second extra point because Penn State was offsides on the first try. Although the team looked offsides on the second try, no penalty was called on the play. The second try was also wide right. The first half ended 13-7 with Penn State scoring on a 38-yard touchdown pass with only seconds left in half. SMU had made a substitution of reserves right before the half and this probably aided Penn State in their late first-half score. In the third quarter, Triplett, who had run behind Doak Walker, caught a six-yard

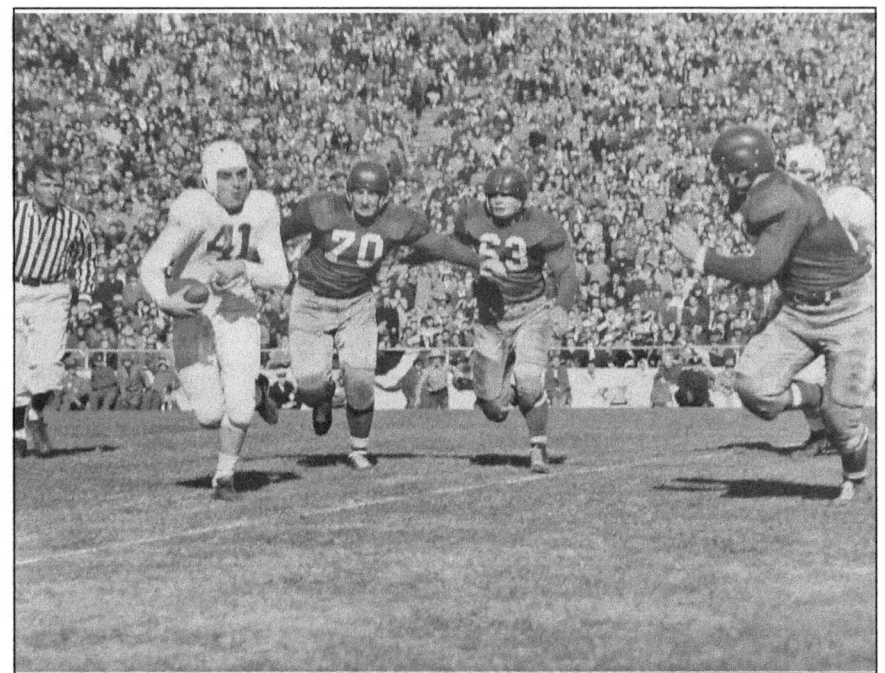

Penn State back Petchel tries to get around Hamberger and Lewis

pass to tie the game. Eddie Czekaj's try for extra point was ruled wide on a delayed call, and the score stood 13-13.

The game ended in a dramatic conclusion with Penn State on SMU's 37-yard line. According to one depiction of the game, Penn State coach, Bob Higgins, thought that his team was behind in the final seconds of the game and that was why Penn State was throwing so many passes. With two seconds to play, Penn State quarterback Elwood Petchel (listed as 5'8", 145 pounds in the game program) was chased toward the right sideline and threw a jump pass into a cluster of players in the end-zone. Dennie Hoggard was in that group of players and closest to the ball but said afterward that the ball was tipped and never reached him. The game ended in a 13-13 tie.

Two key players in the game, SMU's Walker and Penn State's Elwood Petchel, had equally impressive game statistics. Their Cotton Bowl statistics reflect the great game day performances by both players.

*Paul Page catches 53-yard pass from Doak Walker for first SMU score*

| Cotton Bowl Statistics, Petchel and Walker | | |
|---|---|---|
| | Petchel | Walker |
| Rushing | 25 yards in 9 carries | 56 yards in 18 carries |
| Passing | 7-15 for 93 yards | 5-9 for 69 yards |
| Touchdowns | 7-15 for 93 yards | 1 Running |
| Extra Points | 0-0 | 1-2 |
| Interceptions | 0 | 1 |

## Game Aftermath

Hoggard recalled after the game that as he was leaving the field, he felt a hand on his shoulder. He turned around and there was Doak Walker. Hoggard recalls that Walker said, "Nice game. You almost won it." Other Penn State players recalled that the pass was a bullet pass that hit Hoggard in the breadbasket and that he should have caught the ball. In response to postgame ribbing from his teammates, Hoggard said, "If God wanted me to catch it, I would

*Frank Payne (right) accepts a 1948 Cotton Bowl Trophy*

have." Not a bad response from the son of a Baptist minister, but the remark sounded more Presbyterian than Baptist.

Wally Triplett, the back, went on to lead Penn State in scoring and all-purpose yards his senior year in 1948. He was the first black drafted player to play in the NFL. Triplett played four years for the Detroit Lions. In 1950, Doak Walker joined Triplett on the Detroit team. Triplett often said he would kid Walker about his Penn State touchdown catch against SMU in the Cotton Bowl that cold and bright January day. Triplett said, "I caught that touchdown pass behind him, and I used to kid him about it."

The box score on the game indicates how close the 1948 Cotton Bowl was statistically. Not only were the players from both teams exhausted after the game, but SMU's mascot, Peruna, did not fare well health wise. Peruna had a high fever and runny nose so was rushed to a horse doctor after the game. Getting Peruna to the doctor also was problematic after the game. The fans were going out of the southeast tunnel of the stadium and had jammed the exit. Peruna was not the loveable little horse that SMU fans always expect to see, and nipped at a few fans and started kicking up her heels. Departing fans quickly opened a pathway for Peruna, and the little horse made a quick departure.

| 1948 Cotton Bowl Statistics | | |
|---|---|---|
| | SMU | Penn State |
| First Downs | 12 | 12 |
| Net Yards Rushing | 92 | 165 |
| Net Yards Passing | 114 | 93 |
| Passes Attempted | 25 | 15 |
| Passes Completed | 11 | 7 |
| Passes Intercepted | 1 | 1 |
| Number of Punts | 7 | 4 |
| Average Distance of Punts | 33.1 | 33.4 |
| Fumbles | 3 | 2 |
| Ball Lost on Fumbles | 1 | 2 |
| Number of Penalties | 1 | 3 |
| Yards Penalized | 5 | 15 |

Another minor incident occurred in the Penn State locker room. A middle-aged male alumnus charged into the locker room and started berating Higgins and the Penn State coaching staff for using poor strategy during the game. Dallas police had to remove the man from the locker room.

On a more cordial note, after the game, both teams gathered at the SMU Student Union Building for what the *Dallas Morning News* called, "an old-fashioned chuck wagon feed." The paper reported players from both teams eating seconds, thirds, and fourths. At the conclusion of the event, all the players received, "their trophies, handsome gold engraved wrist watches, and Cotton Bowl blankets."

## Game Follow-Up

With few exceptions, SMU students were happy with the results of the 1948 Cotton Bowl game. However, some supporters were not quite as happy with the SMU marching band. The following letter appeared in the *SMU Campus* newspaper in the "Letters to the Editor" of January 10, 1948, edition.

> Dear Sirs:
>
> "The Nationally Famous Mustang Band"!!! Is your caption under the picture on Page 7 of the January 7th issue sarcasm? If not, it should be — but then maybe not, for no doubt the band is nationally famous for being the joke of the Southwest Conference.
>
> After the exhibition of the White Oak High School at the Cotton Bowl, the Mustang Band should have been ashamed to proceed with their amateur routine. White Oak didn't share honors with SMU. They stole them. Completely. Let's have a better band and less bragging. If we earn it, our horn will be tooted by others, and then the band will be "nationally famous."
>
> SMU Supporters

In the same edition of the *SMU Campus* was an article that described how Matty Bell and the SMU football coaching staff were going to the National Football Coaches Association meeting in New York. The purpose of their visit was to advocate doing away with the extra point in college football on a one-year trial basis. Bell thought college football would be more exciting without the extra point. He also was pushing for unlimited substitution during college games.

But the most important write-up to follow the 1948 Cotton Bowl was the following *SMU Campus* article published on January 7, 1948.

## The Real Victory

"New Year's Day saw history made in the annual Cotton Bowl contest. Fans witnessed evenly matched teams engage in a hotly contested battle without victor or loser. Mustangs may be justly proud of the outstanding sportsmanship and playing ability exhibited by the SMU eleven. But there was something even more important.

For the first time, white and Negro athletes played against each other in a major sports event in the south. Contrary to the fears of many that some unpleasantness might arise before the afternoon was over, Penn State's two Negro grid men played with hardly any heckling from the many thousands of spectators. And, apparently, the playing field itself was equally free of any injured feelings.

Cotton Bowl officials, the SMU coaching staff, and the Pony eleven should be congratulated for their courage and honesty in refusing to allow prejudices to stand in the way of bringing to the bowl contest the best possible opponent – Penn State. The Lions, too, are due praise for accepting the invitation when they weren't certain as to how the mixed team would be received here.

Yes, it was truly a great game with plenty of thrills for everyone, but it is possible that the details of the grid battle will someday be forgotten while fair-minded people everywhere still will remember the more important victory which took place that New Year's Day in the minds and hearts of men."

# Chapter Eleven
# More Than Just a Game

**The Loneliest Losers — "Why hasn't the NCAA
dropped the death bomb again?
Much of the answer lies in the athletic rubble at SMU."**

*"If the death penalty was intended to change a place forever, then it has succeeded here. SMU is chastened and fearful, with modest expectations. There is no place quite like it in college football. Probably never will be again."*

Illustration by Tom Bauer (Based on "End of the Trail" sculpture by James Earl Fraser). The illustration appeared in an article by Tim Layden in Sports Illustrated titled "The Loneliest Losers."

*"Still the gold standard for cheating in college football, the SMU Mustang football program of the early and mid-1980s was the poster child for the renegade Southwest Conference and general college football lawlessness."*

Starting in the late 1950s, the culture of America began to change at a faster pace. Not that a changing culture is good or bad for society, but different. Historical events over time, changes in technology, changes in climate and weather, and changes in health and nutrition all affect societies. American sports and American colleges and universities that administer college football programs also changed over seventy years. Colleges and universities spend millions of dollars on football practice facilities alone. Upgrading or building new football stadiums costs millions of dollars. One might ask what these expenditures have to do with providing students a better college education. To the average college football fan, the myth of the football student-athlete disappeared twenty years ago. There is no college sport that has fundamentally changed more in the last seventy years than college football. Appendix C highlights many of the differences between 1947 football at SMU and football at SMU in 2015.

The biggest change in college football, however, is not observable in the statistics of Appendix C. There are different football rules, formations, and uniforms. The biggest change in college football, however, is the effect of the National Football League (NFL) on its minor league – college football. The National Football League has the highest attendance of any professional sports league in the world and is the most popular professional sports league in America. In 2016, the NFL made $7.1 billion in revenue. The current eligibility rule states that a player must be out of high school for three years to participate in the NFL draft. Most high school recruits who have professional football aspirations would not even consider attending a college or university that does not have a top-tier college football program. Playing at a school, such as SMU, which is in a non-power conference, is viewed by many players as hurting their chances to be drafted by the NFL.

## SMU 1987 Death Penalty

The 1987 SMU death penalty is on the mind of every SMU football fan. It is a flashback that occurs at every close game loss, every football season below .500, and every signing day when an expected "Five Star" high school recruit changes his mind on a commitment to SMU and commits to a college football program elsewhere. The 1987 NCAA football death penalty will always affect SMU football. The other football experience that affected SMU football fans the most was the SMU football season of 1947. The SMU 1947 team had one of the best college football players of all time and gave Dallas football fans a high that they would not experience for another twenty-five years. That next Dallas football high was the Dallas Cowboy's first Super Bowl win in 1972.

SMU football got caught up in a time of the Southwest Conference of "do whatever you have to do to win." During the late 1970s and early 1980s, an all-Southwest Conference tackle could make about $50,000 a year in unreported income. Almost all the money received was in cash. Other monetary perks were in the form of non-traceable gifts or highly paid summer jobs with little to no work performed. Throw in an occasional professionally paid woman and a Firebird from a forgotten elderly aunt, and a new college football recruit in the Southwest Conference had a clear path to the NFL. With most of the Southwest Conference schools providing extra benefits to their players, the smaller schools in the conference, like SMU, also provided additional benefits to many of their players to remain competitive.

The circumstances regarding the situation of SMU's football program were that SMU had been penalized on five separate occasions and was found to be cheating again when on a current probation. The other factor the NCAA considered in their decision was the arrogance of SMU in fighting against the NCAA regarding SMU's transgressions. The NCAA had enough and handed down the 1987 death penalty on the Ponies. The penalty included canceling the entire 1987 season, revoking fifty-five scholarships, and reducing the number of assistant coaches from nine to five. SMU also decided to cancel the 1988 season.

## "Pick the Mustangs; They're a Safe Bust"

The question still lingers. Yes, the Ponies were guilty, but did SMU deserve the death penalty? It has been a one-time football death penalty in the NCAA. Why just SMU? The timing of the penalty is part of the answer. In an article in The *Dallas Morning News* on June 12, 1981, Skip Bayless wrote a prophetic statement on the future of SMU football titled "Meyer marked man from the beginning." Bayless quoted Russ Potts, the SMU Athletic Director as saying, "Some people want to see you do well but not too well. If you're 6-5, you're OK, but 8-3 and a Holiday Bowl berth?" In the following year 1981, with Ron Meyer coaching, SMU was 10-1-0, and in 1982, Meyer was gone.

In 1985, Randy Galloway, of the *Dallas Morning News*, also predicted bad times ahead for the Ponies. On September 19, 1985, Galloway wrote, "The NCAA which left no jock strap unturned in its pursuit of violations at SMU, won't even talk to a man who testified under oath in a federal court about violations with Texas A&M?"

## A History of Football Probations

In 1953, the NCAA started punishing college football programs for violating rules and regulations that ranged from recruitment violations to violations regarding the running of the football programs. The Mustangs' first probation occurred in 1958 and more followed. A listing of those NCAA football probations for SMU is as follows:

The Ponies top the poll as the dubious "No. 1" of cheating the most at college football. The Mustangs have been sanctioned by the NCAA seven times for a total of seventeen seasons. The No. 2 spot is taken by Southern California, followed by Auburn at No. 3. Since 1953, the Ponies have spent 28% of their football seasons on probation. Regarding bowl bans, SMU and Auburn both have been banned from bowls nine times. Auburn's bans were part of four sanctions, and SMU's bans were part of five sanctions.

At the printing of this book, SMU is currently under probation in men's basketball and golf. The expiration date for these probations is September 29, 2018.

| NCAA Football Probations for SMU ||||
|---|---|---|---|
| Violation Occurred | Probation Year(s) | No. of Seasons on Probation | Bowl Ban Year(s) |
| 1957 | 1958 | 1 | None |
| 1963 | 1964-1965 | 2 | 1964-1965 |
| 1970-1975 | 1974-1976 | 3 | 1974-1975 |
| 1978-1980 | 1981-1982 | 2 | 1981 |
| 1981-1984 | 1985-1987 | 3 | 1985-1986 |
| 1984-1986 | 1987-1990 | 4 | 1987-1988 |
| 1995-1998 | 2000-2002 | 2 | None |

## The Solution for Sports Cheating at SMU

The solution for cheating at college athletics at SMU is simple. As far as the current athletic coaches at SMU are concerned, little can be done contractually because of the contracts currently in place. In the future, however, there should be a clause in all SMU head coach's contacts that reads:

> Should the head coach or any of his assistant coaches be found guilty of a NCAA violation that results in the NCAA probation or sanction of that SMU sport, the following actions will occur. Southern Methodist University will immediately fire the head coach and all assistant coaches of said sport. Also, the head coach of the SMU sport on NCAA probation or sanction will pay back to Southern Methodist University one year of his or her base salary. There will be no payout by SMU of funds remaining on said coach's contract, and no compensation will be made to a coach because of his or her termination.

If SMU administrators and coaches can't stop cheating, drop that intercollegiate sport at SMU.

# Chapter Twelve
# The Leakage of Time

*"Remember the good times; they are smaller in number and easier to recall. Don't spend too much time on the bad times. Their staging number will be heavy as lead on your mind."*
— *Willie Nelson*

Doak Walker statue on SMU Campus

*"Things have changed at SMU. Gone are the days of a Heisman Trophy Winner, Blue Shirts, the Pony Express, Manada, and Lambda Chi Alpha."*
— *Roy Hohl, Gamma Sigma #717, 1968 SMU Graduate*

Seventy years have passed since the SMU football season of 1947. Almost all of the 1947 team and many of the 1947 SMU football spectators have died. SMU has changed as a University; Dallas has changed as a city.

College football has changed the most of any college sport during this seventy year period. The only question that seems to remain concerns the future of NCAA football at Southern Methodist University. Before we hypothesize as to what that future might be, let's look at five factors that SMU President Gerald Turner should consider before making a change to the current SMU football program.

## No Future Heisman Winners and National Championships

SMU needs to be part of one of the NCAA football power conferences to be considered for a national football championship. For the many reasons listed in Chapter 1 of this book, SMU is different from the university it was seventy years ago. The closest SMU has come to a Heisman winner and a National Championship was in 1982 with Eric Dickerson and an SMU team that finished 11-0-1. That year was thirty-five years ago.

**Solution:** The first step, SMU joins one of the five NCAA football power conferences.

## No Broad Support by the SMU Student Body or the SMU Dallas Alumni

If you didn't go to SMU football games when you attended SMU, there is a good chance you will not go to SMU football games as an alumnus.

A small number of SMU students go to the games, and there appear to be a lot of options for students to occupy their time on game days. In the 1960s, almost all the students went to the Cotton Bowl for the weekly Saturday SMU football game. SMU played familiar opponents or a Southwest Conference team that SMU had played continually for at least thirty years. Another factor, as mentioned in the 2016 *Rotunda*, is that 7% of the current SMU student body is from a foreign country. The students probably are aware of basketball or baseball, but the game of football might be something different. A foreign student might ask, "Are those guys playing rugby out there?"

**Solution:** SMU pays the SMU students and alumni to come to the SMU football games.

## No Broad Support by SMU Professors or Staff

Since the Death Penalty of 1987, the SMU faculty and staff have been lukewarm at best regarding SMU football. Some SMU professors even have told their students not to go to SMU football games and hit the books instead. In 1947 SMU football was king, but in 2015 SMU football is just another sport, take it or leave it.

Schools that have had the most successful programs in college football are the schools that, for the most part, were successful fifty years ago. Football tradition plays a big role in big-time college football today. Professors at tradition-rich universities tend to be more supportive of their programs because of the money and prestige that comes with a successful NCAA Division I football program.

**Solution:** The Ponies win 50 football games in a row by whatever means possible.

## No Broad Support by the Dallas Community

In looking at pictures of home games of SMU football in 1947, the stadiums appear to be full. The average number of filled seats at SMU home football games in 1947 was 32,750. The average attendance for home football games in 2015 was 21,043. Currently, there are a lot of empty seats at the majority of SMU home football games. It should be noted that college football attendance is usually based the number of tickets sold and not the number of fans that attend a game.

One major reason for empty seats at Ford Stadium is that the SMU football program is sandwiched between two highly successful football programs. On one side of the football spectrum is Highland Park High School. Highland Park is one of the most successful high school football programs in the state of Texas. The Scotties have won 801 games, the most wins of any high school in the state. Highland Park also has a record number of fifty-eight playoff appearances in the state. The Scotties current head coach Randy Allen is number four on the list of all-time winning high school football coaches in Texas, with 361 wins in thirty-six seasons. In 2016, Highland Park was the state champion in Texas Class 5A-Div2 football.

On the high side of the football spectrum is the juggernaut, the Dallas Cowboys. The Cowboys are the highest valued professional sports team in the world. The stadium has been sold out for every game since the opening of AT&T Stadium in 2000. In 2016, the Cowboys had four of the top five best-selling jerseys in the NFL, and the Cowboys still heavily market the moniker "America's Team." In 1978, the famous narrator of NFL Films, John Facenda, opened an NFL highlight film with "They appear on television so often that their faces are as familiar to the public as presidents and movie stars. They are the Dallas Cowboys — America's Team."

Although the Dallas Cowboys slipped last year to No. 2 in the NFL team popularity poll, it hasn't affected the Cowboys overall popularity. Anyone who lives in Dallas, Texas, and wants to be socially accepted better be a Dallas Cowboys fan. If someone boasts of being an Eagles or a Packers fan at an informal social gathering, he might as well leave the function or be left standing there talking to himself. The majority of local Dallas TV stations lead with a Dallas Cowboy story even into the NFL off-season. The *Dallas Morning News* rarely mentions the SMU Football Mustangs. To find a story on the SMU football team in The *Dallas Morning News*, you need to turn to the back page of the sports section and work your way forward.

Many of the 1947 SMU football fans interviewed for this book were given the question, "What one thing has hurt the success of SMU football the most in the last forty years?" The same answer by all alumni that answered this question is the Dallas Cowboys.

**Solution:** Jerry Jones moves the Cowboys to Little Rock or Los Angeles.

## Rising Costs of the SMU Athletic Programs

SMU administrators never mention the current cost of the SMU football program and the financial effect the SMU football program is having on the university. If SMU President Gerald Turner was not as successful in raising funds for SMU, it is likely that the football program at SMU might have closed down years ago. One factor that might have saved the football program several years ago was a small group of wealthy boosters called the "Circle of Champions." Around 2012, this group of boosters donated substantial funds to SMU football and other SMU sports programs. The headline of an article in the May 1, 2012, *Daily Campus* read, "Athletics deficit still on the rise." The article noted the high cost of SMU athletics and the lack of access to the athletic department's financial statements for both the students and the Daily Campus. But just how much money goes to intercollegiate sports at SMU? Mackenzie O'Hara of the *Daily Campus*, wrote:

> A 2010 NCAA report examined the athletic department budgets of SMU and the other 119 Football Bowl Subdivision (FBS) schools. Ninety-eight lost money. Between 2007 and 2010, the median annual deficit for these colleges was about $9.6 million. During the same period, the SMU athletic department lost $18.6 million annually — nearly twice the median deficit of the other schools.

Dan Orlovsky, the 2012 faculty chair of SMU's athletic policies committee, commented with "SMU's comparatively high losses are a result of little television money, low attendance at football games, high expenditures in recent years and travel expenses."

Also, around 2010, an added SMU cost was the amount the university paid for big-name football and basketball coaches. When asked about the terms of his contract with SMU, then head basketball coach Larry Brown said," I've always been overpaid, and this is no exception."

**Solution:** Moving to a NCAA Division II football program, would substantially reduce the annual cost of SMU football.

## Is It Football Decision Time?

Is SMU going to make changes regarding their football program? A college can turn around a basketball team, a golf team, or soccer team with one or two great players and a good to exceptional head coach. A positive change to a college football program is much harder to do and can be a much longer process than any other sport.

There are three basic decisions that SMU President Gerald Turner could make regarding the football program at SMU today.

## Close the SMU Football Program

Until big money boosters decide to throw in the towel, the current football program will remain. The only other possible scenario is that Turner steps down and the new SMU president decides it is time to pull the plug.

## Leave the Football Program as Is

This decision has the highest probability of happening among the three choices. Two factors could change this decision: (1) no indoor football practice facility is built and (2) head football coach Chad Morris leaves SMU and goes to A&M.

A new University President also could drive a change to a new view of football at SMU. But, another ten years of the same SMU football results and SMU alumni might not care if there is an SMU football program.

## Take the SMU Football Program to Division II

An obvious and seldom-discussed solution is to move the football program to a Division II status. In discussing this move with the NCAA, the organization advised me that a two divisional college or university is allowed but must be sanctioned by the NCAA. All the other SMU sports programs would remain as Division I programs. A reason that the NCAA might allow this to occur at SMU is that the NCAA owes SMU a little mercy. If the NCAA can give a school the "death penalty," the NCAA can allow a split on the NCAA divisions of their sports programs.

In October 2009, the Knight Commission issued a report on intercollegiate athletics that focused on NCAA football. The Commission reported some interesting and intriguing findings:

"The myth of the business model — that football and men's basketball cover their expenses and fully support non-revenue sports — is put to rest by a NCAA study finding that ninety-three (of the then 119 FBS institutions) ran a deficit for the 2007-08 school year, averaging losses of 9.9 million."

"Proponents for men's sports have long said that sports opportunities for men diminish as slots for women have grown because of Title IX, but many studies have found otherwise."

"There is no correlation between spending more on athletics and winning more ... And increased spending on coaches' salaries has no significant relationship to success or increased revenue."

"... on average institutional subsidies to athletics are rising faster than educational subsidies for the student body."

SMU President Gerald Turner has served on the Knight Commission. Because of serving on the Commission, President Turner is probably aware of the foreword to the 2009 report:

"This report sets forth reforms that are achievable and that, if implemented, will create a foundation upon which future reforms can build. Our blueprint for restoring educational values and priorities begins with strengthening accountability for intercollegiate athletics in three ways:

1. Requiring great transparency and the reporting of better measures to compare athletics spending to academic spending;

2. Rewarding practices that make academic values a priority;

3. Treating college athletes as students first and foremost and not as professionals."

# Conclusion: The Best SMU Football Season

The 1947 SMU Football season is rapidly disappearing into the past and the forgotten.

Those who played in sporting events and observed as spectators in the stands remember football games the best. Seeing a football game on TV doesn't count, as you just must be there. As no-loss seasons become more and more a rarity in college football today, there is a tendency to diminish the teams of the past that went undefeated. The timeline of college football contains too many variables to ever compare players and a team from 1947 to players and a team in 2015. The 1947 fans can compare what they saw on the SMU football field in 1947 to what they have seen on the SMU football field in the 70 years since.

A trait of the 1947 SMU fans interviewed for this book is that they all have a deep devotion and love for Southern Methodist University. Health permitting, the 1947 fans still attend SMU football games. If those fans live in Dallas, they also commit to attending as many SMU sporting events as possible. It could be that these 1947 fans are seeking to catch a glimpse of a running back who can run like Doak Walker, intercept passes like Paul Page, throw like Gilbert Johnson, or block or tackle like John Hamberger.

The future of SMU football is impossible to predict, but looking at the past seventy seasons of SMU football, it has been hard to find an SMU team with the character and heart of the 1947 SMU football team. The 1947 team also had Doak Walker, who might have been the greatest college football player of all time.

The 1947 SMU football season was "Glory on the Hilltop."

# Postscript
# The Reality of the 2015 SMU Football Season

*"I think SMU will win at least four or five football games this season."*

— Buster Brown, lifelong SMU football fan whose father, Melville Marshall Brown, was an SMU football letterman in 1928. (August 2015)

It is September 26, 2015. My SMU football season tickets are in Section 114 of Gerald J. Ford Stadium on the Southern Methodist University campus. As I enter the stadium, once again I am aware of the vast number of empty seats and the nearly empty SMU student section in this 42,000-seat stadium. Most of the SMU games over the last couple of years average about 400 students in attendance. This number is based only on my casual observation from having attended SMU home football games over the past seven years, since the opening of Ford Stadium. There are lots of empty seats in Ford Stadium, even though SMU's current undergraduate student enrollment is approximately 6,700 students. My seats are in the end-zone section because, in that location, a season ticket is approximately

$100 for six or seven SMU home football games. The price is a bargain because after the game begins, I can sit almost anywhere in the stadium. Low attendance at most SMU home football games means there are lots of empty seats in Ford Stadium, which is a one-tier football stadium with the playing field below ground level, allowing for a great open view of the playing field from almost any seat in the stadium.

I make my way to the second row from the top of Section 214, but I move quickly across to Section 212. Section 212 has a better visual angle of the field of play.

When I arrive at my seat, the only fans within thirty seats of me are a young SMU graduate wearing a heavily worn SMU sweatshirt and his pudgy girlfriend, who is showing more of her ample, tattooed and pierced body than should be shown in public. As the game begins, the couple seems more enamored with themselves than the game on the field and spends a lot of time going back and forth to the concession stand for beer and oversized pretzel sticks.

Today, as usual, the speakers on the scoreboard of Ford Stadium are set at their typical high volume. The music is hip-hop, which the SMU football players and the students like, but the old, white SMU alumni have no interest in hearing or understanding this music that is outside the cultural zone of North Dallas, where most SMU alumni reside. Even to my aged ears, the beat of "Turn Down for What" can be a little too much when played at an eardrum-breaking volume and repeated a dozen times during the game. Meaningless electronic replays also lengthen the game time. The average fan never knows who is doing the questioning or why the play is under review. Numerous TV timeouts also add about three to four minutes of dead time for the fans in the stands. During the time outs, fans get the pleasure of being subjected to commercials on the jumbo screen or a dose of the hip-hop music at a high-volume level. Rarely does the Mustang band play, except at half time or during the thirty seconds before the snap of the ball.

SMU alumni also get pitched to give more money to the University during games. Like many colleges and universities in America today, SMU is relentless in its campaigns asking for money, buildings, landscaping, facility chairs, tennis courts, or swimming pools. As tuitions continue to rise at astronomical rates, the need for more funds has never been greater. Even a college graduate can't understand the correlation between tuition costs and fund raising. Alumni receive phone calls from current students, letters from college deans and President Turner, and emails from distinguished alumni and classmates asking for some financial return for the great knowledge the alumni received in Hyer Hall twenty-five years earlier. A casual observer might get the impression that the great University on the Hilltop might be more interested in raising money (for whatever purpose) than providing a quality education to their current students.

Today's game with James Madison unfolds like most of the 2015 SMU football games, with SMU taking an early first-half lead and then either being beaten like a drum in the second half or losing the game in the last couple of minutes or seconds of the fourth quarter. The outcome of the James Madison/SMU game would come down to the last thirty-seven seconds. As the 2015 season drags on to a 2-10 closure, many SMU alumni wonder if season ticket holders are getting their money's worth. How long will it take for head coach Chad Morris to turn around the SMU football program and return to the glory days of June Jones? SMU football super fan Buster Brown was only off his pre-season prediction by two games. Many disappointed SMU football fans search for a reason why another football year of great promise has turned out so bad. Is the reason an evil spell conjured up by the NCAA? Or is it the lingering effect of the 1987 death penalty? When will another starting SMU quarterback leave the SMU program to become successful at another college? When will another exit quarterback become successful in the NFL? Could Hayden Fry (SMU head football coach 1962-1972) cast an evil curse? Even though his record was a semi-respectable 49-66-1, Fry was fired by SMU and went on to coach at the University of North Texas and Iowa University. In 2003, Fry was inducted into the College Football Hall of Fame.

As I sit in the stands of a half empty stadium during this beautiful early fall afternoon, my mind begins to wander, especially during TV timeouts. But luckily, not all my mental wanderings are related to SMU football, even when sitting in the SMU stadium during a game.

## Personal Days on the Hilltop

Personal student experiences at SMU are the basis for some wanderings. One such wandering is that I went to all the 1966 SMU home football games and the 1966 SMU/Georgia Cotton Bowl game with my girlfriend at the time. She was the perfect women for a male in his senior year at SMU in the late 1960s. With an outgoing and engaging personality, she became the Sweetheart of Lambda Chi Alpha Fraternity years later. She was strong-willed, knew what she wanted, and knew how to have a good time, but she had her limits. She set the limits in our short relationship as well. Her favorite phrase during a year and half of dating was, "We're not ready for that yet." From a twenty-year-old male's perspective, her persona was one that I could never fully understand or appreciate. Several years later, the failed relationship started to make sense.

Her two best features were great looking legs and beautiful lips. I could kiss those lips for hours and never want to stop. Unfortunately, beautiful co-ed lips significantly lowered my SMU GPA. Two additional attributes were beautifully shaped, over-sized breasts (a three-hooker was needed to hold them in place) and her ability to consume large quantities of beer at fraternity parties or pubs near SMU. One of our favorite college activities was to spread a blanket on the shores of White Rock Lake and consume a six pack or two of the King of Beers. We also would devour four or five packages of Nabisco animal crackers to help absorb the alcohol from St. Louis' best. With a slight buzz, we would return to our respective fraternity and sorority houses. A male friend later said, "Some women you can read like a book, but others you can't get beyond the cover, and sometimes the book is in a language you can't completely comprehend or understand."

Singer Jimmy Buffett, perhaps, explains male relationships with women the best in his song Margaritaville. "Some people say there is a woman to blame, but I know it's my own damn fault."

## Past Glory Years

My second reflection is always of the glory years of the SMU Pony Express. The SMU teams in the early 1980s were some of the best teams' money could buy in college football. There were numerous stories of Pontiac Trans Ams with suitcases full of cash hidden in the car's trunk. The Trans Ams never were parked but always were seen driving aimlessly around the SMU campus. Cash is better when it is on the move. But cash was never a problem in the old Southwest Conference to players, fans, or alumni. A friend who pitched for the Texas Longhorns baseball team in the early 1970s said that after he pitched a good game for the Longhorns a $50 bill would magically appear on the top shelf of his locker.

But all the talk of money, cars, and women could not take away the fact that SMU had several seasons of football teams that were the most talented teams in the country. Between 1980 and 1984, SMU had the highest winning percentage (.839) of any Division I-A school in the country. As I sat in the stands in the Dallas Cowboys' Texas Stadium, there was always the chance that Eric Dickerson "…could go all the way!!!" But even in the early 1980s, few SMU home football games were sellouts. Opposing Southwest Conference fans always turned out in large numbers and were noticeably vocal in their support for their teams and universities. An enthusiastic female Arkansas fan that I knew would harass me at SMU home games against Arkansas. She would call out on a bullhorn, "Sit down Williams, your team sucks." The Pony Express's best year was 1982 when the team won the Cotton Bowl and finished No. 2 in the country with an 11-0-1 record. The Pony's 17-17 tie was to Arkansas, in Arkansas, in the last game of the year.

## Death Penalty

Reflection No. 3 is more like a never-ending bad dream that doesn't have a wake-up alarm. All the great potential and expectations came to an end when SMU football died on February 25, 1987. That day, more than the music died. SMU football died in the NCAA message of "Death to the Ponies." Former SMU quarterback, "Dandy" Don Meredith, often is quoted as saying, "If ifs and buts were candy and nuts, we'd all have a Merry Christmas." What direction would have SMU football gone if they hadn't been given the death penalty in 1987? In alternative universe thinking, there would be no death penalty in a parallel world. SMU football would have taken an entirely different path in its football program. Maybe the Ponies would have been NCAA national champions at least a couple of times during the 1980s or 1990s without the death penalty.

John Gribbin's excellent book, *In Search of the Multiverse* describes the theory of alternative universes and hidden dimensions. David Berlinski offers a counter opinion in his book, *The Devil's Delusion*, which questions the validity of string theory. How absurd is the possibility of as many as twenty-three different dimensions?

But returning to the reality of the universe in which we currently reside, after going to hundreds of SMU football games over the past twenty-seven seasons, I think about the SMU death penalty at every SMU football game that I attend. The SMU death penalty is talked about by fans and alumni on the SMU Boulevard before almost every home game. The death penalty is discussed after every spring football signing day via emails among SMU alumni. The death penalty also is questioned every fall by my barber, Troy Tipton, who asks me, "How will the Mustangs do this coming season?" My numerous ex-SMU fraternity brothers living everywhere from Hawaii to Atlanta, Georgia, ask the same poignant question every year, "What is wrong with this years' Ponies?"

I'm always on the defense with the SMU death penalty issue at family gatherings, when University of Texas family exes asks, "Why can't SMU recruit better football players? Why did June Jones unravel? Why is attendance so low at SMU football games?" The answers my questioning friends are still out there "blowing in the wind." However, one common answer to every lingering SMU football question is the SMU football death penalty of 1987.

## Down Years

And finally, as the last musing of a game day reflection, there is the factor of the importance of winning. It has been stated hundreds of times over the last fifty years that America loves a winner and Dallas, Texas, loves a football winner even that much more.

The one major exception is the Dallas Cowboys, who have not won a Super Bowl in the last twenty years. But the Cowboys are on the front page of the sports section of the *Dallas Morning News* almost every day of the year. Forty years of subscribing to the *Dallas Morning News* leads me to this observation. The Cowboys have sold out AT&T Stadium every game since the opening of the stadium. This attendance record occurred even when the Cowboys had several losing seasons. Cowboys fans seem to have a love/hate relationship with Cowboys' owner Jerry Jones. The Cowboy fans thought Tony Romo was the messiah of NFL quarterbacks. Even though Romo never even won a divisional NFL championship, there is already a fan campaign to place Romo in the Cowboy Ring of Honor.

Only seven of the nineteen coaches in the history of SMU football has had career-winning records at SMU. Since 1960, there have been only sixteen winning SMU football seasons. The worst years in this down stretch were the three seasons of 1989 thru 1991. In this period, the Ponies won just four games. During these years, I had two season tickets on the fifty-year line and attended every home game. When SMU had its first winning season after the down stretch, the price of my season tickets doubled and my parking cost quadrupled. I wrote a short note to SMU President Gerald Turner explaining my displeasure with the increases. The good President was quick to respond that the SMU Athletic Department sets football ticket and parking prices. However, the next football season found me sitting in the north end zone of the stadium, musing about the great fifty-yard line seats I had enjoyed for those three seasons.

## Game Over

Over the last few football seasons, I usually have not stayed until the end of an SMU home football game. The James Madison/SMU game on September 25, 2015, was different. The game was back and forth for the entire game. SMU's quarterback, Matt *Davis*, had a good game in both his passing and running. He was 18-30 with 262 yards passing and one touchdown, and 17 rushing attempts for 95 yards and two touchdowns. But alas, the Pony defense could not hold. The Dukes rolled up impressive 729 yards of total offense. The game ended when the Dukes' quarterback Vad Lee found John Miller with a 17-yard touchdown pass with just 27 seconds to play. The final score: James Madison 48 and SMU 45.

The game also ended a streak of three home games where SMU topped 20,000 fans in attendance. In the final four home games of the 2015 SMU season, the attendance at Ford Stadium averaged 16,885. No one knows how many SMU undergraduate students attended these four games.

# Appendix A

| 1947 SMU Football Roster | | | | | | |
|---|---|---|---|---|---|---|
| **Player** | **Age** | **Pos.** | **Wt.** | **Ht.** | **Hometown** | **Class** |
| John Basham | 19 | T | 205 | 6:0 | Fort Worth | Jr |
| Lloyd Baxter | 24 | C | 195 | 6:2 | Sherman | Sr |
| Kenneth Blackburn | 22 | BB | 200 | 5:11 | Dallas | Soph |
| Raleigh Blakley | 23 | E | 195 | 6:0 | Dallas | Soph |
| Wayne Burnett | 23 | E | 187 | 6:0 | Tyler | Jr |
| Louis Burress | 24 | WB | 195 | 6:3 | Dallas | Soph |
| Harold Clark | 19 | E | 210 | 6:4 | Dallas | Soph |
| Earl Cook | 22 | G | 217 | 6:2 | Dallas | Sr |
| G.B. Cranfill | 20 | C | 180 | 6:0 | Groesbeck | Jr |
| Dick Davis | 21 | G | 180 | 6:2 | Dallas | Soph |
| Bobby Duke | 18 | FB | 165 | 5:10 | Dallas | Soph |
| Joe Ethridge | 19 | T | 210 | 5:10 | Kermit | Jr |
| Bobby Folsom | 20 | E | 185 | 6:0 | Dallas | Soph |
| Fred Goodwin | 21 | C | 190 | 6:0 | Dallas | Soph |
| Kenneth Grantham | 21 | TB | 158 | 5:9 | Pampa | Soph |
| John Gray | 22 | BB | 183 | 5:9 | Galveston | Soph |
| Ed Green | 25 | WB | 180 | 6:0 | Gainesville | Sr |
| Jack Halliday | 19 | T | 220 | 6:3 | Dallas | Soph |
| Sid Halliday | 25 | E | 195 | 5:11 | Dallas | Sr |
| John Hamberger | 23 | T | 220 | 6:1 | Dallas | Jr |
| Claud Hill | 22 | T | 202 | 5:10 | Goose Creek | Sr |

## 1947 SMU Football Roster

| Player | Age | Pos. | Wt. | Ht. | Hometown | Class |
|---|---|---|---|---|---|---|
| Gilbert Johnson | 24 | TB | 180 | 6:2 | Tyler | Soph |
| Henry Johnson | 19 | T | 194 | 5:11 | Atlanta | Jr |
| Jimmie Kendrick | 21 | WB | 165 | 5:10 | Dallas | Jr |
| Walter King | 20 | T | 215 | 6:4 | Atlanta | Jr |
| Floyd Lewis | 24 | G | 202 | 5:11 | Jefferson | Jr |
| Eric Lipke | 21 | G | 210 | 5:11 | San Antonio | Soph |
| Grady Martin | 24 | E | 205 | 6:5 | Silverton | Jr |
| Dick McKissack | 21 | FB | 195 | 6:2 | San Antonio | Soph |
| Zohn Milam | 23 | E | 190 | 6:0 | Eliasville | Soph |
| Billy Mizell | 19 | FB | 180 | 6:0 | Ennis | Jr |
| David Moon | 19 | BB | 190 | 6:1 | Mart | Jr |
| Cecil Moseley | 24 | G | 175 | 5:10 | Dundee | Soph |
| Sammy Owen | 19 | WB | 160 | 5:9 | Gladewater | Jr |
| Paul Page | 20 | WB | 180 | 6:2 | Eldorado | Jr |
| Carroll Parker | 24 | WB | 195 | 6:2 | Sapulpe | Sr |
| Howard Parker | 21 | BB | 225 | 6:2 | Tyler | Soph |
| Frank Payne | 19 | TB | 165 | 6:0 | Breckenridge | Soph |
| Julius Pechal | 26 | G | 195 | 6:0 | LaGrange | Sr |
| Francis Pulettie | 25 | BB | 205 | 6:1 | Waco | Jr |
| Bob Ramsey | 23 | BB | 195 | 5:11 | Dallas | Sr |
| Dick Reinking | 20 | E | 180 | 6:1 | Dallas | Sr |
| Eddie Richardson | 22 | C | 210 | 6:0 | Tyler | Sr |
| Walter Roberts | 22 | G | 198 | 5:11 | Pelly | Soph |
| Gene Roberts | 21 | TB | 165 | 5:10 | Teague | Fr |
| Melvin Rosenblum | 20 | G | 205 | 6:2 | Brooklyn | Sr |

| 1947 SMU Football Roster |||||||
|---|---|---|---|---|---|---|
| Player | Age | Pos. | Wt. | Ht. | Hometown | Class |
| Norman Rosenblum | 25 | T | 36 | 6:1 | Brooklyn | Sr |
| Bill Sullivan | 18 | FB | 195 | 6:3 | Dallas | Fr |
| Cecil Sutphin | 23 | C | 175 | 6:3 | Baytown | Sr |
| Herbert Wales | 18 | G | 190 | 6:0 | Dallas | Soph |
| Doak Walker | 21 | TB | 170 | 5:11 | Dallas | Soph |
| Carl Wallace | 19 | E | 165 | 6:0 | Dallas | Soph |
| Bill Weatherford | 19 | TB | 165 | 5:10 | Dallas | Soph |

# Appendix B

| SMU Football Demograpics | | |
|---|---|---|
| | 1947 | 2015 |
| Number of Campus Buildings<br>• Permanent<br>• Temporary | 26<br>26 | 102<br>0 |
| Student Enrollment<br>(1947 Total Enrollment, 2015 Undergraduate) | 6,830 | 11,643 |
| Male/Female Student Ratio<br>(1948 Sr Class, 2015 Undergraduate) | 67% Male<br>33% Female | 50% Male<br>50% Female |
| % of Foreign Students<br>(1948 Undergraduates, 2015 Total Enrollment) | 0.004% | 14% |
| Minority Makeup of Student Body<br>(1949 Sr Class, 2015 Total Enrollment) | 0% | 27% |
| President's Annual Salary | Lee: $12,000 | Turner: $3,254,128 |
| Schools of the University | • Theology<br>• Business<br>• Engineering<br>• Music<br>• Law<br>• Arts<br>• Science | • Theology<br>• Business<br>• Engineering<br>• Arts<br>• Law<br>• Humanities<br>• Science<br>• Education<br>• Human Development |

# Appendix C

| SMU Football Demograpics | | |
|---|---|---|
| | **1947** | **2015** |
| Head Football Coach's Salary | Bell: $6,000 | Morris: $2 million+ |
| Stadium Capacity (Ownby, Ford)<br>Cotton Bowl | 23,783<br>45,504 | 32,000 |
| Home Attendance<br>1947: 4 Games;<br>2015: 7 Games | 131,000 | 147,301 |
| Number of Players Listed on the Team | 66 | 157 |
| Cost of a SMU Game Football Program | $0.25 | $5.00 |
| Cost of an SMU Game Football Ticket | $2.00 | $24 to $289 |
| Average Weight of a Lineman* | 207 | 285 |
| Average Weight of a Back* | 185 | 204 |
| Highest Weight of a Player* | 220 | 325 |
| Basic Cost of a Cotton Bowl Ticket | $4.40 | $225.00 |
| *Only starting football players | | |

# Appendix D

## SMU Home Attendance Comparison

| 1947 Home Games | |
|---|---|
| Opponent | Attendance |
| Missouri - Cotton Bowl | 35,000 |
| Rice University - Ownby Stadium | 23,000 |
| University of Texas – Cotton Bowl | 50,000 |
| University of Arkansas – Ownby Stadium | 23,000 |
| Total | 131,000* (Average 32,750) |
| **2015 Home Games** | |
| Baylor | 32,047 |
| University of North Texas | 25,401 |
| James Madison | 22,314 |
| East Carolina University | 17,136 |
| Tulsa | 18,217 |
| Temple | 17,232 |
| Tulane | 14,954 |
| Total | 147,301 (Average 21,043) |

Ownby Stadium (Capacity 23,783)
Cotton Bowl (Capacity 45,504)
Gerold Ford Stadium (Capacity 32,000)
*Total does not include attendance of 47,500 at 1948 Cotton Bowl game against Penn State

# Acknowledgements

Frank Payne and John Hamberger, the only two 1947 players interviewed for *Glory on the Hilltop*, contributed greatly to the book's content and photographs. Both men eloquently described their playing for the Ponies seventy years ago. Also, Payne and Hamberger reflected on their continued love of SMU and how the 1947 SMU football season affected their lives after playing for the Ponies so long ago.

Also, I wish to thank Tasos Pappadas, a 1947 cheerleader, for inviting the author into his Houston home. He not only discussed the 1947 season but also described his working with Coach Hayden Fry in helping to recruit future Mustang players when Fry coached at SMU.

Without the support and guidance provided by the staff of the DeGolyer Library at Southern Methodist University, much of the material in *Glory on the Hilltop* would not have been available. The following staff members of the University Archives were of great assistance by providing requested SMU sports and general SMU information:

Katie Dziminski, Head of Public Services
Anne E. Peterson, Curator of Photographs
Kendra Wilson, Archival Assistant
Terre Heydari, Operations Manager

Also assisting in research and providing information on SMU campus life in 1947 was SMU's University Archivist, Joan Gosnell. Over the one and half years of writing *Glory on the Hilltop*, Ms. Gosnell has provided valuable suggestions to the author as to what material might be of interest to readers. Gosnell also gave suggestions on where to find material related to the culture and economics of America immediately after World War II. But most of all, Ms. Gosnell provided inspiration to bring *Glory on the Hilltop* to completion.

The author also wishes to acknowledge Jay Miller, Executive Director, of Student Media Company, Inc. The loaning of *Rotunda*s and past articles from the *SMU campus* newspapers greatly enhanced the content of *Glory on the Hilltop*.

I am also grateful to Gerry York, Manager of SMU Heritage Hall, for his time in providing names and contact information of individuals who lived through or are related to those individuals who experienced the 1947 SMU football season. Without the input from these interviewed individuals, the recollections of the 1947 football season described in *Glory on the Hilltop* would have lacked detail, clarity, and insight into the 1947 SMU football season.

I also acknowledge those interviewed individuals who provided the author with their recollections of the 1947 SMU football season. Thanks to Brad Bradley, Patty Bell Kendrick, Darrel Lindsey, Norma Peterson, Patsy Newman, and Carolyn Page Price.

And finally, the following individuals proofed and made suggestions as to content on selected chapters or *Glory on the Hilltop* in its entirety: Frank Payne, John Hamberger, Tasos Pappadas, Patty Bell Kendrick, Joan Gosnell, Charles Ketz, Roy Hohl, Margaret Williams, and Michelle Morse.

# Sources

## Books
1947 *Rotunda*, SMU Yearbook, Student Media Company.
1948 *Rotunda*, SMU Yearbook, Student Media Company
2016 *Rotunda*, SMU Yearbook, Student Media Company.
*Doak Walker: More than a Hero*, Masters Press, 2647 Waterfront Parkway, East Drive Indianapolis, Indiana 46214. Whit Casering, Dan Jenkins, 1997
*Doak Walker: Three Time All American*, The Steck Company, Austin Texas. Dorothy Kendall Bracken as told by Doak Walker, 1950
*In Honor of the Mustangs*, Darwin Payne, 2010.
*Kings of the Hilltop*, Gene Wilson
*Mustang Mania*, Temple Pouncey, The Strobe Publishers: Huntsville, Alabama 35801, 1979.
*Old Centre*, 1919 Centre College Yearbook.
*Old Centre*, 1920 Centre College Yearbook.
*One Hundred Years on the Hilltop*, Darwin Payne
*SMU 1982 Pony Express*
*Talent is Overrated*, Geoff Colvin, Penguin Group, 2008.
*The Old Centre*, 1917 Centre College Yearbook.
*The Perfect Pass*, American Genius and the Reinvention of Football, S.C. Gwynne, Scribner - An Imprint of Simon and Schuster.
*Twelve Mighty Orphans*, Jim Dent

## Pictures were obtained from the following sources.
1948 Cotton Bowl Football Program, pages 12, 137
1948 *Rotunda* (SMU Yearbook), Student Media Company, pages 54, 56, 58, 60, 61, 64, 66, 68, 71, 75, 78, 84, 108, 110, 112, 114, 115, 123, 128, 129
Frank Payne Jr., pages 79, 120
Joe Redwine Patterson, pages 41, 93
Pam Locher, Back Cover
Robert Hurst, pages 88, 90, 91
Tasos Pappadas, pages 81, 87, 94
T.R. Williams, pages 46, 48, 89, 155
SMU Archives, DeGolyer Library, pages 1, 3, 4, 29, 32, 33, 35, 37, 43, 62, 69, 72, 77, 82, 83, 85, 86, 96, 97, 100, 101, 103, 105, 116, 121, 131, 133, 136, 141, 142, 143, 144, 145
SMU Flash Photography, page 49

SMU Heritage Hall, pages 22, 34, 52
*Sports Illustrated*, page 149

## Magazine Articles
"Doak, the greatest football player that ever lived, lives" by Mark Goodman, *Esquire Magazine*
"The Loneliest Losers" by Tim Layden, *Sports Illustrated*

## The SMU Campus
*The SMU Campus*, Volume 33, Number 1, September 7, 1947
*The SMU Campus*, Volume 33, Number 2, October 1, 1947
*The SMU Campus*, Volume 33, Number 3, October 4, 1947
*The SMU Campus*, Volume 33, Number 4, October 8, 1947
*The SMU Campus*, Volume 33, Number 5, October 11, 1947
*The SMU Campus*, Volume 33, Number 6, October 15, 1947
*The SMU Campus*, Volume 33, Number 7, October 18, 1947
*The SMU Campus*, Volume 33, Number 8, October 22, 1947
*The SMU Campus*, Volume 33, Number 9, October 25, 1947
*The SMU Campus*, Volume 33, Number 10, October 29, 1947
*The SMU Campus*, Volume 33, Number 11, November 1, 1947
*The SMU Campus*, Volume 33, Number 12, November 6, 1947
*The SMU Campus*, Volume 33, Number 13, November 12, 1947
*The SMU Campus*, Volume 33, Number 14, November 15, 1947
*The SMU Campus*, Volume 33, Number 15, November 19, 1947
*The SMU Campus*, Volume 33, Number 16, November 22, 1947
*The SMU Campus*, Volume 33, Number 17, November 26, 1947
*The SMU Campus*, Volume 33, Number 18, November 28, 1947
*The SMU Campus*, Volume 33, Number 19, December 3, 1947
*The SMU Campus*, Volume 33, Number 20, December 6, 1947
*The SMU Campus*, Volume 33, Number 21, December 6, 1947
*The SMU Campus*, Volume 33, Number 22, December 13, 1947
*The SMU Campus*, Volume 33, Number 23, December 18, 1947
*The SMU Campus*, Volume 33, Number 24, January 1, 1948
*The SMU Campus*, Volume 33, Number 25, January 7, 1948
*The SMU Campus*, Volume 33, Number 26, January 10, 1948
*The Daily Campus*, Volume 88, Number 69, January 23, 2003
*The Daily Campus*, Volume 96, Issue 89, May 1, 2012
*SMU Campus Weekly*, Volume 101, Issue 22, February 4, 2016

## Newspapers

"Dallasite lifted cheerleading as sport, business" from staff and wire reports, *The Dallas Morning News*, Sunday July 5, 2015.

"Game Change: SMU set new course by playing against black athletes" by Jeff Miller, *The Dallas Morning News*, February 26, 2010.

"Growth of Cotton Bowl" by Jere R. Hayes, Sports Editor, *The Dallas Times Herald*, January 1, 1948.

"Lions and Mustangs Both Content with Tie after Grueling Tussle" by Harry Gage, *The Dallas Morning News*, January 2, 1948.

"Lions and Mustangs Split Cotton Bowl Honors, 13-13" by George White, *The Dallas Morning News*, January 2, 1948.

"Long Runs Spice Play of Ponies" by George White, *The Dallas Morning News*, September 28, 1947.

"Meyer marked man from the beginning" by Skip Bayless, *The Dallas Morning News*, June 12, 1981.

"Mustangs Defeat Steers in Nerve Thriller, 14-13" by George White, *The Dallas Morning News*, November 2, 1947

"Mustangs Hard Pressed to Beat Hogs 14-6" by Felix R. McKnight, *The Dallas Morning News*, November 16, 1947

"Mustang Pass Defeats UCLA Bears 7-0" by George White, *The Dallas Morning News*, October 26, 1947

"Mustang Passes Dazzle Texas Aggies 13-0" by George White, *The Dallas Morning News*, November 9, 1947

"Nittany Lions Head Home with Trophy," *The Dallas Morning News*, January 3, 1948

"Ponies Outclass Rice to Win 14-0 Upset" by George White, *The Dallas Morning News*, October 19, 1947

"Ponies Rally Late, Down Bears, 10-0" by George White, *The Dallas Morning News*, November 23, 1947

"Ponies Trip Pokes 21-14" by William T. Rives, *The Dallas Morning News*, October 12, 1947.

"Shaking Pompoms for the Grandfather of Modern Cheerleading" by John Branch, *The New York Times*, March 15, 2009.

"Walker's 56 Yard Run Prevents TCU Victory" by Felix R. McKnight, *The Dallas Morning News*, November 30, 1947.

"Walker Sparks Ponies' 35-19 Win Over Tigers" by Felix R. McKnight, *The Dallas Morning News*, October 5, 1947.

"Where was the NCAA back in '83?" by Randy Galloway, *The Dallas Morning News*, September 19, 1985.

"Who in the Heck was Paul Page?" by Chris Turner, *San Angelo Standard Times*, August 27, 1995.

| Contacted Individuals | | |
|---|---|---|
| **Name** | **Connection** | **Contact Date** |
| Bradley, Brad | SMU Sports Photographer | Nov. 15, 2016 |
| Gosnell, Joan | SMU University Archivist | June 3, 2016<br>March 3, 2017 |
| Hamberger, John | SMU Class of 1949<br>1947 Team Member | Sept. 19, 2016<br>Dec. 1, 2016 |
| Hurst, Robert C. | Son of I.T. Hurst | Feb. 11, 2017 |
| Hurst, Betsy Weber | SMU Class of 1978 | Feb. 11, 2017 |
| Kendrick, Patty Bell | SMU Class of 1952<br>Daughter of Matty Bell | Jan. 3, 2017<br>Sept. 25, 2017 |
| Lindsey, Darrel | SMU Class of 1949 | July 24, 2015 |
| Mangrum, Dr. Robert | Howard Payne University Historian (Email) | April 10, 2017 |
| Morgan, Beth | Centre College Historian (Email) | April 11, 2017 |
| Newman, Patsy | SMU Class of 1955 | Oct. 18, 2016 |
| Pappadas, Dr. John | Son of Tasos Pappadas | May 2, 2017 |
| Pappadas, Tasos | SMU Class of 1948 | May 23, 2017 |
| Patterson, Joe | SMU Class of 1949 | Jan. 6, 2011<br>April 5, 2011<br>June 26, 2012<br>Aug. 25, 2012 |
| Peterson, Norma | SMU Class of 1948 (Phone Interview) | Feb. 6, 2017 |
| Payne Jr., Dr. Frank | SMU Class of 1950<br>1947 Team Member | Sept. 15, 2016<br>Sept. 14, 2017 |
| Price, Carolyn Page | Daughter of Paul Page (Phone Interview) | April 14, 2017 |
| York, Gerry | SMU Class of 1958 | Aug. 15, 2016 |

# Index

**A**
Allen, Randy, 158,
Andrews Sisters, 8

**B**
Baker, Dr., 9
Baker, Harrison, 2
Baugh, Sammy, 17, 34
Bayless, Skip, 152
Bednarik, Chuck, 17
Bell, Dr. Clayton, 27
Bell, Matty, v, 16, 24, 29-35, 99, 100, 102, 117, 122, 126, 129, 131, 138-140, 147
Bell, Matty, the dog, 63
Berker, Lloyd, 138-139
Berlinski, David, 170
Berman, Chris, 69
Berry, Raymond, 62, 132
Blair, Janet, 141
Blakley, Raleigh, 124, 173
Brown, Buster, 165, 167
Brown, Dorothy, 95
Brown, Larry, 42, 48, 159
Brown, William L., 125
Bruce, A.D. Jr, 125
Buffett, Jimmy, 168

**C**
Callahan, Chris, 135
Campbell, Dave, 101
Campbell, Leon, 126-127
Canaday, James, 121
Carty, Rico, 38
Casanova, Bill, 108
Chappus, Bob, 12, 24
Chenault, Tom, 168
Cherry, Blair, 23
Chuckran, John, 140
Clark, Harold, 52, 140, 173
Collins, Bobby, 107
Colvin, Geoff, 106

Cook, Earl, 114, 129, 139, 173
Cox, Christina, 48
Crowley, Bill, 108
Czekaj, Ed, 140, 143

**D**
Davis, Matt, 171
Doughty, Brandon, 135
Dent, Jim, 40, 101
Dickerson, Eric, 24, 156, 169
DiMaggio, Joe, 8
Driver, Charles, 94

**E**
Eikenberg, Virgil, 114
Ekmark, Fred, 58
Ellis, Kirby, 44
Ethridge, Joe, 52, 66-67, 114, 173

**F**
Facenda, John, 158
Feitler, Gloria, 85
Folsom, Bobby, 52, 110,
Forbis, Buddy, 41
Fry, Haden, 23, 33, 35, 94, 167, 183
Frye, Hugh, 87

**G**
Galloway, Randy, 152
Garrett, Keyarris, 135
Gibson, Pat, 62
Gillespie, Tyler, 122
Gillroy, Byron, 122
Gobel, Jim, 87
Grange, Red, 17
Green, Ed, 52, 110, 112, 126, 173
Grey, Gilman, 41
Gribbin, John, 170
Griffith, Andy, 11, 19
Groom, Winston, 64, 65
Gwynne, S.C., 34

## H

Halliday, Sid, 52, 58, 59, 112, 173
Hamberger, John, 6, 18 53, 61-64, 141, 143, 163, 183-184
Hamberger, Sarah, 64
Hanna, Rod, 27
Hawn, Fritz, 73
Hayworth, Rita, 8
Henry, Derrick, 135
Herkimer, Lawrence, 81, 85-86, 88, 95-98, 107
Higgins, Bob, 140, 143, 146
Hill, Claud, 140
Hoggard, Dennis, 139, 143-144
Hohl, Roy, 67, 155, 184
Hughes Al, 85
Hurst, I.T., 46, 81, 86, 89-92, 189
Hurst, Robert, 189
Hutson, Don, 17

## J

Jenkins, Dan, 42
Johnson, Gilbert, 51, 52, 73, 75-76, 105, 112, 117, 122, 124, 127, 163, 174,
Jones, Jennifer, 47-48
Jones, Jerry, 171
Jones, June, 167, 170

## K

Kelly, Tom, 38
Kendrick, Patty Bell, 139, 184
Kenton, McAdoo, 16

## L

LaGrone, John, 62
Lamberty, Ed, 38
Landry, Tom, 63, 122
Layne, Bobby, 13, 23, 114, 121-122
Leach, Bobby, 120
Lee, Vad, 171-172
Lewis, Floyd, 64-65, 114, 143, 174
Lewis, John, L., 71
Lindley, Darrel, 9
Lively, Bill, 27
Locher, Pam, 168

Lucas, George, 46
Luckman, Sid, 8
Lujack, Johnny, 12, 24
Lundquist, Verne, 27

## M

Mace, Alex, 47
Malloy, Joan, 58
McKissack, Dick, 52, 60, 105, 109, 112, 119, 121, 122, 127, 142, 174
McKnight, Felix R., 126
Meredith, Don, 136, 169
Meyer, Dutch, 32, 33
Meyer, Ron, 152
Meyers, Robert, 30
Miller, Jay, 46
Miller, John, 172
Moore, Marc, 87
Morris, Chad, 16, 95, 160, 167, 179
Movie, Wizard of Oz, 3
Moxley, Bill, 52, 112, 140

## N

Nelson, Willie, 155
Newman, Anna Bell, 85
Newman, Pat, 90, 184, 189
Neyland, Robert, 17
Nolan, John, 140

## O

O'Hara, Mackenzie, 159
Orlovsky, Dan, 159
Orsini, Steve, 45-46
Oswald, Lee Harvey, 38

## P

Page, Paul, 25, 52, 72-74, 105, 117, 119, 124, 127, 129, 142, 144, 163, 174
Page, Wilson, 72
Pappadas, Eunice, 95
Pappadas, John, 189
Pappadas, Tasos, 81, 86, 93-95, 116, 183, 189
Patterson, Amy, 44

Patterson, Ann, 44
Patterson, Caroline, 40
Patterson, James, 40
Patterson, Joe Isham, 39
Patterson, Joe Jr, 39, 44
Patterson, Joe Redwine, v, 24, 37-50, 51, 81, 85-92, 95, 107, 114, 116, 123, 125, 131, 132, 141
Patterson, Julian, 40
Payne, Frank Jr., 51, 52, 53, 76, 77-79, 105, 112, 119, 124, 139, 145, 183, 189
Payne, Frank Sr., 77
Petchel, Elwood, 143, 144
Peters, Ray, 128
Peterson, Norma, 26, 140-141, 184, 189
Petty, Paul, 41
Pickett, Wilson, 92
Porter, Wesley, 85
Potsklan, John, 140
Potts, Russ, 152
Pulatti, Francis, 76

## R

Ramsey, Bob, 52, 54-55, 71, 174
Ray, Harlan, 73
Reinking, Dick, 52, 71, 121, 124, 174
Rice, Grantland, 26
Rockne, Knute, 19
Romo, Tony, 171
Rudin, Johnny, 87
Russell, Jane, 109
Russell, Rusty, 16, 18, 52, 62, 72, 99, 100-102

## S

Sanford, Mary Lou, 85
Scott, Clyde, 126-128
Shafer, Terry, 169
Shaw, Gary, 95
Sisco, Jack, 126, 128
Smith, Blane, 120
Snavely, Carl, 18
Spelling, Aaron, 41-44, 87
*Sports Illustrated*, 150

Stollenwerck Elizabeth Ann, 141
Stuckey, Lewis N., 1-2
Suhey, Steve, 139
Sutphin, Cecil, 52, 68-70, 138-139, 175

## T

Tartt, Blake, 81, 86, 90, 92-93, 107
Taylor, Harry, 119
Thornton, Duval, 127
Thorpe, Jim, 17, 18
Tipton, Troy, 170
Todd, Harold Hart, 2
Torres, Jake, 47
Townsend, Johnny, 135
Trespalacios, Ramon, 47
Triplett, Wally, 139, 142, 145
Turner, R. Gerald, 10, 156, 159-161, 167, 171, 177
Tusa, Joe, 116

## W

Walker, Doak Jr., v, 13, 17, 18, 21-27, 52, 73, 78, 79, 81, 83, 95, 108-113, 117, 119-120, 122, 124, 126, 129, 132, 133, 135, 163, 175,
Walker, Doak Sr., 23
Wallace, Carl, 52, 116, 175
Warner, Glenn "Pop", 18
Warner, Skeeter, 27
Whitaker, Bill, 21
White, Allie, 101
White, Dr. Lori, 45-46
Williams, Ted, 8
Wolosky, John, 138
Wood, Bill, 41

www.ingramcontent.com/pod-product-compliance
Lightning Source LLC
Chambersburg PA
CBHW050526170426
43201CB00013B/2103